John Doughty

The Parable of Creation

Being a presentation of the spiritual sense of the Mosaic narrative as contained in

the first chapter of Genesis

John Doughty

The Parable of Creation

Being a presentation of the spiritual sense of the Mosaic narrative as contained in the first chapter of Genesis

ISBN/EAN: 9783744797528

Printed in Europe, USA, Canada, Australia, Japan

Cover: Foto ©Lupo / pixelio.de

More available books at **www.hansebooks.com**

THE
PARABLE OF CREATION,

BEING

A Presentation of the Spiritual Sense of the Mosaic
Narrative as contained in the

First Chapter of Genesis,

— BY —

Rev. John Doughty,

Author of "The World Beyond," "The Garden of Eden,"
"The Secret of the Bible," etc., etc.

∴

SAN FRANCISCO:
SWEDENBORG LIBRARY AND TRACT SOCIETY,
1626 O'Farrell Street.
1892.

PREFACE.

There can be no doubt that a large portion of the prejudice against the Bible which is held by skeptical minds comes, not so much from wilful infidelity as from misunderstanding. The same may be said of the present tendency among all Christian sects to deny the plenary or verbal inspiration of that book which claims, in itself, to be the Word of God. It is not because people want to reject it so much as because they cannot discern wherein its inspiration, in many parts, consists.

The method of interpretation revealed by the Lord through Emanuel Swedenborg and set forth in the Writings of that illumined expositor, discloses the fact that it is only in its spiritual sense that the Word of the Lord can be made fully consistent, harmonious and rational, and be justified, as such, to spiritual minds.

These lectures, delivered in San Francisco, Portland, Or., and other places, to large audiences, were designed to set forth the spiritual meaning of the Mosaic account of creation, as given in the *Arcana Coelestia* of Swedenborg, in a form so easy to comprehend, that none might fail to understand who were willing to listen in an unprejudiced mood. They, of course, give the spiritual sense of a very small portion of the Scripture; but they at least suggest the reasonableness and beauty of that method of interpretation and may serve to lead the interested mind to investigate further, and nearer the fountain head, for the principles upon which it is founded.

SAN FRANCISCO, March 1st, 1892.

J. D.

CONTENTS.

I
Out of the Darkness into the Light, - - - - 9

II
The Heavenly Firmament, - - - - - - 32

III
First Spiritual Fruits, - - - - - - - 55

IV
The Elevation of Love and Faith, - - - - 78

V
The Living Soul, - - - - - - - - - 101

VI
The Image of God, - - - - - - - - 124

VII
The Sabbath of Rest, - - - - - - - 146

I.

OUT OF THE DARKNESS INTO THE LIGHT.

In the beginning God created the heaven and the earth. And the earth was without form, and void; and darkness was upon the face of the deep. And the Spirit of God moved upon the face of the waters. And God said, Let there be light: and there was light. And God saw the light, that it was good: and God divided the light from the darkness. And God called the light Day, and the darkness he called Night. And the evening and the morning were the first day.—Gen. 1: 1-5.

One error is usually the parent of a thousand. False premises inevitably lead to false conclusions. A single flaw in the logic of an argument is subversive of the truth of all succeeding statements. A mistake in one figure at the beginning of a protracted arithmetical calculation will grow into an error of millions in the outcome.

This law is universal. Error will not, in any of its aspects, produce truth. There is only one royal rule for the pursuit of wisdom, and that is to *start* from facts or propositions which are true. In that case we at least begin aright with a fair prospect of so continuing; while otherwise we begin wrong with a certainty of diverging further and further into error at each succeeding step.

The subversion of this rule has constituted the grand trouble of Christian doctrine. It is this which has divided churches, created sects, aroused the din of conflicting opinions, and rent Christendom into a hundred warring fragments. It is this which has placed weapons in the hands of infidels wherewith to wound the church, has furnished them with arguments for the overthrow of its truths, and has presented to them fair opportunities for ridicule.

It is this which has disgusted honest seekers after truth, and repelled the many whose minds are so constituted that they cannot decide between conflicting opinions which are equally unfounded, nor accept of dogmas which offend their rationality.

No illustration of this could be more obvious than that which may be made by the estimation which has been placed upon the Bible. That book is held to be the Word of God. It is regarded as a revealment of his will, and an embodiment of his wisdom. So far it is well. But as a fundamental principle of its construction, we are further informed that it is to be literally construed; that it has no higher purpose than appears upon its face; that its histories are mere human histories, its allusions to creation and other kindred themes literal geological science; and the inconsistencies of its letter, mysteries beyond the reach of the human mind, to be acknowleged by faith.

This is the error which has been the parent of all perversions of the Bible. Paul says that "all scripture is God-breathed." He admonishes his brethren that God has made them able ministers, not of its letter but of its spirit. And he warns them that "the letter killeth, but the spirit giveth life." So it is his delight to extract from sacred history its true spirit. He has little use for its letter, except to draw from narrative or ceremonial command a spiritual explanation which shall lead his hearer's mind, away from the earthly things of which they seem to treat, up to the holier lessons with which he shows them to be full.

In this he does but follow the example of our Lord. Whether in quotations from the old Scripture or in sayings of his own, our Lord ever leads the mind above the letter, above the earthly, to the spiritual lesson with which the literal is filled. Without a parable—without a spiritual meaning within the literal saying—it is declared that He never spake to them. In this manner the water of Jacob's well became a lesson of that spiritual water—the gospel truth—of which he who drank would live forever. In this way the story of the destruction and upbuilding of the temple became, at his lips, a history of his own death and resurrection. Thus the miracle of the multiplication of the loaves and fishes became, under his explanation, an illustration of the truth that men were to labor for the meat which endureth unto everlasting life. And when his disciples were inclined grossly to misunderstand the command that they were to eat his flesh and drink his blood, He declared to them, "It is the Spirit that quickeneth, the flesh profiteth nothing."

But why multiply examples? The literal sense of the Scripture is valueless except as it contains, enwrapped within, a spiritual lesson. The Word of God has been made of none effect by the process of literalizing it. This fundamental error has sapped its life, has made it seem inconsistent, and has taught by implication that God had no higher motive in giving the Old Testament than to write a history of the Jews, and no grander purpose in the opening of Genesis than to inform us of the manner of earth's creation. Thus has error rendered the Divine Word a mystery to its believers, and a derision to its enemies.

The fundamental truth which restores to the Bible its true character is, that it is throughout a book of spiritual wisdom. It ought not to be otherwise believed than that when God undertakes to give a revelation to man, his design is to communicate to him knowledge concerning those things which man by his natural powers has no means of learning. Thus He would not seek to teach man history, geography or science, because these are things which man may learn by the exercise of his natural faculties of observation, investigation and reason. It is also better that man should learn them for himself, because, by so doing, he developes his rationality, judgment and manhood, which, were all knowledge miraculously given of the Lord, would remain undeveloped.

But there is a certain line of truths—those which relate to God, heaven and eternal life, which are beyond discovery by mere natural study or deduction. They cannot be thought out from any principles of earthly science, nor evolved from any inner consciousness formed from a life in the world. They can only be learned by revelation from God. Consequently when the Lord gives a revelation to man, it is and must be concerning those higher and more hidden things of which he can learn in no other way. If the Divine mind inspire a book it will thus be worthy of its infinite authorship, and will teach concerning God and his nature, the future life, and the means of reaching the highest blessings which that life affords. It would be derogatory to the character of the Divine mind, to attribute any other design to the books which are to constitute the Word of God to man.

Why should God inspire a history of the wars of the Jews and the cruelties they practiced? Why a narrative of the abominations of the heathen nations of Canaan? Why should he miraculously give forth an account of creation which, from a scientific point of view, is in no wise equal to that which the rude rocks of earth have themselves revealed? Only because they have higher meanings than error has been in the habit of admitting; only because the parable is always God's chosen method of spiritual utterance; only because they were written neither as history nor as science; not to teach the one nor to enforce the other, but to use outward narrative forms for the expression of interior spiritual truth.

In this view we approach the Mosaic account of the creation. It was not divinely inspired as a scientific treatise but as a spiritual allegory. It is not fitted together as a consistent geological formula of natural facts, but as a weaving of the order of earth's development into a spiritual parable. Its expressions are not worded in scientific form, and its statements are not rendered with scientific precision; but both are so arranged according to the divine law of correspondences, and after the method of sacred symbolism, as to effect the spiritual purpose designed.

So if it lacks philosophic precision, if it fails in scientific accuracy, if it is somewhat inconsistent with modern geology, it is because it has no relation to science. Its symbols are correct. its correspondence is clear, its spiritual meaning true. It is in this latter fact that its divinity resides. It is in this that it becomes worthy of its Divine origin. For this and not the other is its purpose, end and use.

It has been clearly shown by scholars that the pecular style of Hebrew in which this and the following ten chapters of Genesis are written, places their origin away beyond the time of Moses. Infidel writers lay great stress on this point, and assert that Moses could not have written them. But they forget that he does not claim to be their author. They ignore the fact, plainly indicated in various portions of Scripture that there were sacred books which constituted a Word of God before Moses wrote and before Abraham was born. These books, though now lost, were in existence in the time of the early scripture penmen, as is evidenced by the fact that by them they are, on several occasions, quoted. The style of the first eleven chapters of Genesis, then, simply shows that they were copied from some more ancient sacred books. How ancient they were no man can tell. It does not matter. But that they are written in the style of sacred symbolism in its purest form--according to that science of correspondences which the ancients understood so well, and that thus they are a continuous parable of spiritual truth, worthy of their origin as a message from God to man, is patent upon their face.

So to him who can see this truth it becomes a matter of indifference how far the history of the creation coincides with the facts of modern science. There are certain general statements here made, of even scientific accuracy, which the Divine Mind has used as a basis for the spiritual parable it sought to evolve; as, for instance, that the development of the earth proceeded by certain progressive and orderly steps, or that it became successively prepared to bring forth certain forms of life—first the lower grades of vegetation, then the higher, then the fish, then the beasts, then man. But having this basis, as there was no design on the part of God to write a scientific treatise, but only to put forth a parable, then the filling in, the forms of expression, the accompanying statements, are in purely symbolic form and style, without the slighest reference to their effect upon the literal meaning of the narrative.

We approach then this first chapter of Genesis as we would approach any other parable uttered by the Lord. We assume that its teaching is spiritual. We do this, because revelation is given only for the sake of making known that which is beyond the natural powers of man to attain. History and science he may gain for himself. He stands in the midst of them and is a part of them. But God, the future world, the science of eternal life, are matters which the natural mind can never learn from the natural world or by natural education, and are therefore subjects for Divine revelation.

Asserting then that its teaching is purely spiritual, what, in the first place, is the general theme of the parable? It is, outwardly, an account of the creation; it must, therefore, be inwardly an account of creation in some spiritual sense.

What then is spiritual creation? Its nature is revealed by the words of David when he said, "*Create* in me a clean heart, O God, and renew a right spirit within me." There is a creation of the natural man, and there is a creation of the spiritual man. The one causes us to live naturally, the other causes us to live spiritually. The apostle Paul alluded to the spiritual creation of the inward man when he said, "Put ye on the new man which is *created* in righteousness and true holiness;" and also in the words, "For we are his (God's) workmanship, *created* in Christ Jesus unto good works." Such men, he called new creatures, that is, new created beings. In this phrase he said to the Corinthians, "Therefore if any man be in Christ he is a new *creature*"—a newly created being. He also called such "renewed" in the spirit of their minds. I.: thus speaking, he did but interpret spiritually and correctly such expressions of the Old Testament

Scripture as these of David: "The people which shall be *created*"—that is those who are regenerated or renewed in spirit—"Shall praise the Lord." "Thou sendest forth thy spirit, they are *created*,"—that is, when the Lord's spirit comes to us we are made holy and righteous.

Thus we see that the terms "creation," and "to create," have, in Scripture phraseology, a spiritual meaning. This renewal of the heart, this cleansing of the spirit, this becoming a new man, was termed by our Lord, the rebirth, or what is the same, regeneration. We have been created or born naturally; we are to be created or born spiritually. Until this second or spiritual birth takes place no man has fulfilled his destiny. We have been created natural beings to live on the earth, we are to be created spiritual beings to live there unto the Lord. This was what our Lord meant when He said, "Except a man be born again, he cannot see the kingdom of God."

The term regeneration, as used by our Lord, (it is a Latin word signifying rebirth) expresses the whole idea. This means that from being worldly minded we are to become spiritually minded; that from being lovers of self and the world we are to become lovers of God and the neighbor. Of the particulars of this change we will learn more further on. We here only note the truth that the history of the creation as given in the book of Genesis is, in its true intent and meaning, a parable of regenertion. Natural creation symbolizes spiritual creation.

But creation is progressive. In this also it is made to typify regeneration. In another parable our Lord has told us how the attainment of the kingdom of heaven, that is, the regeneration of the soul, is a progressive work. It is like a grain of mustard seed, which a man—the Lord—took and sowed in the earth—in the human mind; which at first is the least of all seeds, in that spirituality at the beginning of our regeneration is very small, but growing, becomes a great tree, in that as regeneration progresses, we become great in spiritual perceptions, power and goodness.

Regeneration then, being progressive, not a thing of sudden attainment, but, like a tree, of slow growth, the six days of creation represent the six general states of life through which each one has to pass before he becomes perfect in the sight of God. The exact distinction between these different stages of spiritual progress we will understand better as we advance in the consideration of the six days of creation. Briefly, we may say here, however, that it is somewhat like the case of one who learns a trade. He must first get a knowledge of the tools he will be required to use; he must then be taught their uses; one by one he must bunglingly practice with them; gradually become more skillful in their exercise; and finally be able with perfect knowledge and skill, to chisel, hammer, saw and plane, and thus to turn out at last, in great variety, beautiful works of mechanical handicraft. The regenerating person must first learn truths of a spiritual nature and their varieties; he must then come into a comprehension of them and of their superior nature and beauty; he must then make his first bungling efforts at a spiritual life; and, gradually growing in an understanding and love of spiritual things, he will at last become an intelligent and affectionate citizen of the kingdom, living in its spirit, and performing its uses in the approval of the Lord. It is by slow degrees of advance only that we come into the perfect knowledge and practice of any thing; and the knowledge and practice of a spiritual life, or regeneration, is no exception to the rule.

But it is said, "In the beginning God created the heaven and the earth." The earth is a Scripture symbol, often predicated of man as a spiritual being, or what is the same, the mind of man; for the mind is the real man. Thus when the Psalmist cries out, "The Lord reigneth, let the *earth* rejoice," he certainly refers, not to the planet on which we stand, but to the *people* who live thereon. Or when Isaiah exclaims, "Hear, O *heavens*, and give ear, O *earth*, for the Lord hath spoken," he refers by the heavens not to the skies above, nor by earth to the globe we inhabit, but by the latter to the *people* of the world, and by the former to that within their minds which is sufficiently heavenly to appreciate what the Lord may utter. In the parable of the mustard seed, when our Lord says that "the kingdom of heaven is like unto a grain of mustard seed, which, when it is sown in the *earth* is the least of all seeds," He means that the doctrine of spiritual truth, when first sown in the *mind*, is at first to that mind the least of all things in importance and comprehension. When the Psalmist says, "Truth shall spring out of the *earth*," he does not mean that truth grows like a vegetable in the ground but that it comes forth from the mind of man.

So *earth*, when used as a Scripture symbol, signifies man or the mind of man, and *heaven* when so used, its spiritual or heavenly degree or plane. When they are used, as in the first verse of Genesis in juxtaposition, or in antithesis, the earth symbolizes the earthly, natural or lower plane of the mind, and the heaven, its heavenly, spiritual or higher plane. In construing this chapter as a parable, therefore, it must be so done throughout. And as the Lord, in giving his Word, would first set forth in parable the subject of regeneration or the spiritual re-creation of man, in its general progressive aspects, He chose the creation of the earth as a fitting natural emblem whereby to express it. It is on the same principle as, when He desired to teach a lesson concerning the manner in which our Lord's word is implanted in the mind and the different mental soils in which it is received, He expressed it by the correspondence of a sower—the Lord, sowing seed—implanting truth, in the earth—the mind of man. When then it is said, "In the beginning God created the heaven and the earth," it is a parable, and it means that in and from the beginning of each one's individual career, the Lord seeks to regenerate his internal and his external man, or what is the same, his spiritual and his natural mind; in other words, his heavenly nature and his earthly nature.

In and from the very beginning God created heaven and earth in each one's nature. There is no one who does not begin the career of life with something of heaven created in him of God. You see that something of heaven in the innocence of the infant, in the beauty of his infantile ways, in the loveliness of childhood, and in its trusting, guileless character. What becomes of these afterward is another question.

In every child's mind there is a heredity from its natural parents and a heredity from the Lord. The latter is what gives him the power of spiritual regeneration. But the Divine heredity is that which first asserts itself in the life of the child. Swedenborg says that the highest and holiest of the Lord's angels have in their keeping these initiaments of mind development as they have place at birth, and on into infancy and childhood. Hence the hard, cruel, natural heredity does not rule in the first budding openings of the child's mental life. But the soft, tender, loving implantations of the Lord, invisibly tended and nursed by his gentlest of angels, breathe around the mental beginnings of one who is destined for immortality. These sweet inseminations and breathings, infused into his first conscious life, remain with him always. They may be covered and concealed by the after developments of his harsher nature, but they remain, nevertheless, as the basis upon which an after life of heavenly character may be built, or as the fountain from whence, when sin has asserted itself, and the clouds of heart-evil hang thick and dark upon the outer surface of the nature, fresh inspirations of heavenly desire, and hope and effort, may be drawn. These remains of infantile states which are so redolent with the perfume of heaven, as we will have occasion, further on, to see, constitute the very elements of our after salvation.

In the beginning God created the heaven and the earth. Place the mind upon this as a symbolic description of the creation of your own spiritual nature. God created heaven within *you* and each of you, at the very beginning of your existence, as well as earth. It is not said that He created the earth and the heaven but "the heaven and the earth," because the heavenly element is developed first, and then the earthly heredity manifests itself. Were the earthly developed first, the heavenly were strangled in its very possibilities, before it had even a chance to gain a foothold.

Next we are told that *the earth was without form and void, and darkness was upon the face of the deep.* This expression, "without form and void," literally translated from the Hebrew, would be rendered "voidness and emptiness." How perfectly this describes us in the beginning of our individual careers, before regeneration has set in. As the earth denotes the natural mind, this expression presents it as, previous to the beginning of the new and spiritual birth, void of all real goodness and empty of all genuine conceptions of spiritual truth. And here let us observe also that before one knows a thing, no matter what it is, he is in darkness with regard to it. Before he understands it, the carpenter is in darkness as to his trade, the artist as to the ideas and methods required to produce a perfect picture, the musician as to the laws of harmony and the means of evoking melody. Mental darkness is ignorance with regard to the subjects on which the mind needs enlightenment. The mind is always said to be in the dark with regard to what it does not know. Spiritual darkness is ignorance, or non-comprehension, of the truths of heaven and eternal life. It exists when the mind knows nothing of the principles or the processes of regeneration. Then also the subject takes no clear form before the understanding. That is to say, earth, or the natural mind of man, is without form and void—so far, at least, as holiness or righteousness is concerned—so far as the kingdom of God as an appreciable affection or truth is concerned. A thick darkness, in relation to these things, rests upon the whole face of the mental deeps of the man.

It is true that we are taught many things concerning religion in childhood. We learn catechisms and Bible verses. Parents instil into us many religious facts, and Sabbath school teachers increase their number. We are taught simple prayers and we sing holy songs. Thus we learn the sacredness of religion, and thus we begin to come into an acknowledgment of the fact that goodness and truth are of a superior nature and of a more sacred character than other things.

But before we learned anything about these matters we were in total darkness. How dark is the mind of the infant! What does it know of the Bible and religion, of the good and the true, of the love of God and man! So dark also is the mind of the adult who has not appreciated what it has been taught, who reviles religion, sneers at the Word of God, calls all conversation about higher things hypocritical cant, and lives for self alone. Thus before regeneration, in all spiritual aspects, is the earth of man's mind without form and void, and thus does darkness dwell upon his mental deeps.

And the Spirit of God moved upon the face of the waters. Well; the first thing that opens his discernment to these matters is a certain movement in his mind, a certain dawning affection for the good, a certain willingness to listen to the true, a certain attention excited, which springs not from himself nor is prompted by any solicitations from without. It is an undefined sensation. It takes the form of an awakening desire for something higher than one has —a desire almost imperceptible to himself so quietly has it come. It is the Spirit of God moving upon the face of the waters.

Waters, in the language of correspondences, signify truths. You know the Lord said to the Samaritan woman, "Whosoever drinketh of the water that I shall give him, it shall be in him a well of water springing up into everlasting life." Water symbolizes there and every where that Divine truth which alone makes men wise unto salvation. So when the

Spirit of God moves upon the face of the waters in the mind of any one, it is when those truths taught in childhood, and stored up well within the memory, are awakened, be it to ever so small a degree, by the mercy of the Lord. That inward movement of life within the mind causes you to see in them what you never saw before—their sacredness, their superiority, their truth. When you see this, it is to you as though God uttered the fiat, "Let there be light."

How delightful it is to awaken to a sense of comprehension, wherein you never comprehended before; to see the truth of that which was previously but a dull cloud upon the memory. Such an experience has perhaps had place with all of you.

Right here, some of you have been in much darkness with regard to the true interpretation of Christian doctrine. With a fuller presentation of the spiritual side of Christian truth, your minds have emerged from confusion and voidness into clear seeing. God has said, "Let there be light," and to you, in the simple phraseology of the symbol, "the light was." Or, to bring it more home to the lesson of regeneration, there was, perhaps, a time when you saw nothing concerning God or good; when spirituality was for you a land of darkness, and your mind was void of real good and empty of genuine truth. But when God said, "Let there be light," there was light, and truth, in some degree, however small, then flashed across your mind, and you acknowledged that there was a God though you understood but little of him, and you felt that his religion was sacred though your appreciation of the fact was small.

That flash of light was the first beginning of your regeneration. And when God, from his eternal throne, looked down within the mind so darkened once, and beheld his first illuminating ray break through its gloomy shadows, then he saw the light and pronounced it good. And then He began to divide the light from the darkness. He brought to bear upon you, inwardly, such influences as to cause you to make a distinction in your mind between present views of truth and former errors, or between the good and the evil, a thing not in all respects clear to you before; or between a religious life and a worldly life, a life of love to others and a life all love of self; in short, between the truth with regard to existence and its objects and value, and the falsities which before had prevailed with you, or the ignorance concerning it in which you were steeped.

And God called the light day, and the darkness he called night. Now God calls, in the Divine language of his Word, this new state of yours, this state of light, the day; but the former state of darkness He terms night. The night-time of the soul is its time of ignorance or falsity; its day-time, its condition of enlightenment.

And the evening and the morning were the first day. The very rudimentary beginnings of this change were as the first gray tints of dawn, which, like evening twilights, though lighter than the night, were but shadows after all. Your first perceptions of spiritual things are always indistinct and dull. But by and by they become clearer and clearer like an ascending sun that ushers in the morn. It is first spiritual evening on the soul; it is then spiritual morning. A day, in scripture symbolism, is a state of mind. This evening and this morning, this first breaking of the spiritual light upon the mind's dark earth, in its beginning shadowy, in its progressions brighter, constitutes with every one his first state of regeneration.

How true this is. All mental progress is from darkness into light; all spiritual progress, from evening unto morning. It matters not that the light now is but a dim glimmering in comparison with what it may be. All success proceeds from first steps; all achievements begin at the beginning. This is only the first day. There is light beyond which now would dazzle the eyes. There are conquests beyond of which now the soul does not dream. The work is only begun. There are five days more—five more grand steps of ascent into the realm of truly spiritual life, and then there is rest; then the full blessing of the Lord descends upon the soul, and heaven is won.

Thus, the opening chapter of God's Word to man is an epitome of the regeneration of the soul— a brief history of the passing stages of its upward way. What could possibly be more divinely appropriate? It is not a narrative of the creation of a poor little earth whereon is spent a mere point of human existence in its great eternity of life; but it is a history of that inward creation of a new will and understanding, in the spirit of which the soul shall live forever. How unworthy of any true idea of a message of God to man the one; how incomparably beautiful the other! The Lord's Word was not designed to chain our contemplations to earthly things—all that surrounds us here has power for that—but to wing the thought in heavenward ways. It carries us not in the currents of temporal things, but it points to those of true eternal interest. Our allotted destiny is the regeneration of the soul. We were born to that end; we are to live in the light of that thought; we are to pass on with all preparations made. And will God set us down to an imperfect lesson in geology when the eternal welfare of the soul is at stake? Let us arise out of such wretched thoughts concerning his words of love, and reach out for loftier aspirations in respect to the wisdom we would ask from Him and for higher conceptions of the dignity of things Divine. So may we study his messages with some apprehension of their grandeur, and gain from his instructions more just ideas of true nobility of soul.

II.

THE FIRMAMENT OF SPIRITUAL THOUGHT.

And God said, Let there be a firmament in the midst of the waters and let it divide the waters from the waters. And God made the firmament, and divided the waters which were under the firmament from the waters which were above the firmament: and it was so. And God called the firmament heaven. And the evening and the morning were the second day.—Gen. 1: 6-8.

THE previous lecture was devoted to a preliminary opening of this subject of the Creation, as set forth in the first chapter of Genesis. We must now, at the risk of some repetition, review the positions therein assumed, weaving in such additional thoughts as will render our further consideration of the theme more easy and clear. We must do this, because new ideas do not at once readily establish themselves in the mind. They may be plainly seen at the moment, but if not firmly fixed they are difficult to reproduce just when they are wanted, or may prove to be so fleeting that they cannot again be easily caught. It is by repetition and re-repetition that they become permanent. Gaining them thus as our own, we proceed with ease to take further steps in the chosen line of investigation which, without such preliminary preparation, would be stupid or wearisome.

The proposition was, in our previous lecture, laid down, that when God undertakes to give a revelation to mankind, his design is to communicate to them knowledge concerning those things which they by their natural powers have no means of learning. Thus He would not undertake to teach man history, geography or science, because these are things which he can learn without revelation by the exercise of his natural faculties of observation, investigation and reason. It is also better that he should learn them for himself; because, by so doing, he developes his rationality, judgment and manhood, which, were all knowledge given immediately from the Lord, would remain undeveloped. The world moves upward and onward, in all natural progress, by the ever restless sphere of study, investigation, comparison and practical appliance. It is by these methods that all earthly things are learned, and being learned, are reduced to practice, and are applied to the use and benefit of mankind. Thus whatever is necessary to happiness and comfort, so far as natural life is concerned, is evolved and supplied by man as of himself.

But there is a world beyond this. Here we live for a few brief years; there we dwell to eternity. There is a God who exists beyond the ken of mere natural sense. He is the Author of all things, while the greatest of men, so far as they can be said to create anything, are the authors of infinitesimally few things. Then, also, there is a spiritual life which is not deducible from any thing of the natural world—not from reason, experience or science. That spiritual life, cultivated here, fits us to become angels hereafter and to live forever in heaven.

Now these things are beyond discovery by natural study or deduction. They cannot be thought out from any principles of earthly science, nor evolved from any inner conciousness formed by life in the world. They can only be learned by revelation from God. Consequently when the Lord gives a revelation to man, it is and must be concerning these higher things of which he cannot know in any other way. If the Divine mind inspire a book which shall be worthy of its infinite authorship, it must teach us concerning God and his nature, concerning eternal life as distinguished from earthly life, and concerning the means of reaching and enjoying the highest blessings which that life affords. It would be derogatory to the Divine character to attribute any other design to the books which form the Word of God.

The Word of God then cannot be a book of natural history or science. It must contain, in its essence, only *spiritual* truth. As history, it must give only a history of the *spiritual* states of the church or man. If, therefore, their surface appearances indicate that it is something else, those appearances must be false. The child might imagine that Æsop's fables were given for the mere purpose of relating curious stories of the conversations of birds and beasts which took place in the long ago, but that does not prove the child to be correct. A belief in error never makes error true. But the well instructed man knows better. He is fully aware that the real design of those fables is to teach a lofty moral by means of a written story.

Much more is this true of the Word of God, of which the fables of Æsop are a faint imitation. History is here used not for the history's sake, but for the sake of the spiritual lesson which lies concealed within it. Geography is used, not to give any lessons concerning the relative situations of the seas, rivers or lakes, cities, countries or mountains of olden times, but because of their adaptability to expressing the relative spiritual situations or states of men. An account of creation is given, not with the idea of furnishing man with an epitome of geological science, but because it forms a fitting dress for the portrayal of the regeneration of man. As all Scripture is given in parables and for the sake of its *spiritual* teaching, a history of creation must be, in its essential meaning, a description of the creation and development of the *spiritual* nature within us. This is called by our Lord, the rebirth, or regeneration.

Regeneration is not a mysterious term; it is simply the development of the spiritual nature. As infants we are born entirely natural. At that period we are without any knowledge of any kind. Our very natural senses have to be developed. We learn to distinguish objects one from another, to form sounds into words of sense, to walk, to talk, only by slow degrees of development. Our rationality is unfolded by a still slower process. It takes us eighteen or twenty years to become women or men, either in stature, wisdom, or rationality,

But having thus learned to be natural men, we have still to learn to become spiritual men. This also is a slow development. Many never develop on to the spiritual plane at all. We have learned to comprehend earthly things; we have still to learn to comprehend spiritual things. For this, however, we study no worldly history or science. For this we go to the Word of God. There, this, and this only, is designed to be taught. There we learn to comprehend the Supreme Being, so far as the finite mind can. God, who has hitherto been to us but a name, becomes, for the first time now, a revealed reality. We begin to look to Him, to love Him and to study Him. We study the life which He would have us lead, the spiritual objects and motives for which we should live, and the genuine spiritual results we should seek to attain. We put these in practice; we weave them into our understandings and lives; or rather, we use the means which the Lord has provided, and the spiritual power with which He has furnished us, to do this. We develop out of worldliness and selfishness into angelhood. We become fitted to live in the eternal mansions of the blessed in the great hereafter, and to perform the uses and live the lives which will be required of us there. Regeneration is the process through which we pass, the work of shunning evils as sins against God which we perform, the radical change of will and thought, of heart and mind, which is made within us, as we gradually emerge from the low plane of merely natural and sensuous existence to the highest levels of life, which is summed up in a state of love to the Lord and the neighbor.

The history of the creation is not natural science but spiritual parable. It is not a revelation of the process of the world's formation; it is a spiritual account of the re-formation of heart and mind. So the six days of creation represent the six general states through which all regenerating persons have to pass. At first our minds are without form and void, and darkness rests upon the faces of their deeps. Totally so is this the case in infancy. Not only is the little one in the dark as to spiritual knowledge, but as to all knowledge. Each man, woman or child is in the deepest darkness as to spiritual things, until they begin to comprehend them. The earth, therefore, being a symbol of the mind of man, its being without form and void, and the darkness that rested on the deep, are expressions which fitly represent the void and formless state of the human mind and its intensely dark condition, before the regeneration of the man begins.

Actual regeneration commences when the mind becomes enlightened as to the superiority of spiritual things over natural. Until this takes place we grope in utter darkness. The Lord has in constant view all the affairs of each and all of us, from the first moment of conception and birth on. While leaving us in freedom, so that we seem to be working along of ourselves and in our own way, He is supervising and overruling in the very least affairs of life. He desires that we shall be regenerated in freedom. No one can be forced to become spiritual. It is not in the nature of things that such should be the case. We were not born so to come into spiritual life. That only is part of our nature which we do voluntarily. An angel is an angel, because, of his own choice, he prefers the good. A devil is a devil, because, of his own choice, he prefers the evil. A man may be forced not to do outward wrong, but there is no good in him unless he avoids the wrong in heart as well as in act, and that of his own free will.

On this account, the Lord, while always leaving us in freedom, still watches sleeplessly our daily steps and thoughts, and places us in such positions, and surrounds us with such situations, and leads us where we will get such and so much instruction, as will give us, each according to his genius and nature, the best opportunities to be led into the light with regard to the superiority of spiritual things over natural. This light usually dawns very slowly, but when it comes, it is to the soul as the fiat of God which has said and has long been saying, "Let there be light!"

So the Spirit of God has been moving upon the face of the mind in every effort that his mercy has made to lead us into an acknowledgment of these grand truths: that God exists, that life eternal is of more value than life temporal, that the soul is of greater concern than the body, that spirituality is superior to worldliness. Then as He has been so long whispering, "Let there be light!" when the light comes He sees that it is good. And then also He divides between the light and darkness; that is He causes to arise in the mind a clear distinction between those false principles of life which, as lovers of the world, we believed in, and those true principles which, as citizens of the kingdom of God, we must now acknowledge. There is the same distinction between the false and the true, the evil and the good, ignorance and knowledge, as there is between darkness and light, and the division between them becomes sharp and clear cut only so far as we perceive that distinction.

The first stage or state of regeneration, then, is described, in correspondences, by the incidents of the first day of creation. It consists in gaining this light, in seeing and acknowledging the superior character of that which is spiritual, in the belief that it is from God, and in the distinction, for the first time made within our minds, between the dark errors of the merely natural and worldly state, and the light of dawning truth which has thus flashed across the soul.

How long this will last, whether we rest in what we have gained, or push on for further spiritual advance, depends on ourselves. It must last for a while as a first state, because we cannot go from one stage of regeneration to another without due preparation.

Like the child at school who is promoted through earnest study from class to class, we go from light to light, from strength to strength, from one position in the kingdom of God to another; and yet in each stage of progress we rest for a while, studying the situation, training our strength, confirming the ideas thus far attained, and preparing ourselves in many ways to take position on yet higher spiritual levels, and to so perform this work that we can stand firmly there with no danger of losing again the vantage ground we have thus far gained. Not that we do this consciously or think to ourselves, "I am doing thus and so in order to promotion to a higher class in the ethics and life of the kingdom," but that it is so effected unconsciously to ourselves. Really and truly it is the Lord who does it all, because He is the instructor, overseer and promoting agent in the entire work, and we are never out of his sight or from under his watchful care for a single moment.

Due preparation thus being made then, due spiritual strength gained, we arise into a new state—a second stage of regenerative experience. This is typified in the biblical narrative by the second day of creation.

And God said, Let there be a firmament in the midst of the waters, and let it divide the waters from the waters. And God made the firmament, and divided the waters which were under the firmament from the waters which were above the firmament: and it was so. And God called the firmament Heaven.

We must remember that the first stage of spiritual progress out of the void and the dark, was a coming into the dawning light of spiritual day. It was only, however, a confused and general acknowledgment of the importance of eternal things. But now there is a firmament created, and that firmament is called heaven. Naturally our minds revert to the skies above. But, naturally speaking, sky is only empty space. It may be filled with auras or ethers or still more delicate forms of æriform matter; but there is no flat surface called sky, like a great dome, painted blue, grey or black. So the idea of waters beneath the firmament may take the form of tangible thought, but that of waters above the firmament by no possibility; for there is no such thing as above the sky; it is sky all the way through into the remotest depths of spacial immensity.

We must leave behind all natural ideas here, and remember that we are considering a spiritual parable. In this sense the allusion is to the firmament of the mind—its heavenly regions, those elevated realms of will and understanding which can think of, comprehend and love heavenly or spiritual things.

Mental philosophers have long ago observed and classified the different faculties of the mind. We know that the mathematical faculty does not enable us to sing, nor the musical faculty run the mental machinery which performs intricate arithmetical problems. We know that the poetic faculty does not build machines, nor the mechanical faculty write poetry. Each faculty does its own work, and when it becomes a controlling quantity, it gives tone to the whole character of the man.

But these are all of the natural mind. They do the work of this world, each in its own sphere. Ascending above them, on a higher mental plane, there is a faculty which takes note of what is above nature. It is the spiritual faculty or mind. When this degree or faculty is in conscious activity, we think of, and interest ourselves in, spiritual things. We leave all earthly affairs—its business, its fashions, its domestic duties, its pleasures, and we soar away into thoughts of the supernal. Here comes in our acknowledgment of, and affection for, God. Here we comprehend the immortality of the soul, and see the certainty of a never-ending life beyond the grave. Here we contemplate the exceeding loveliness of a spiritual life, of all those commands which lead to it, of those states of mind which grow happy in its presence. Here we love good and hate evil. Here we reflect upon the goodness of the Lord and realize our trust in Him. Here we worship, praise and pray. Here is our soul's heaven above; while worldly thoughts and states are our earth beneath, This is the firmament which previous to the beginning of our regeneration, when our mind was void and dark, we caught not a glimpse of, and in its first stage, when we were rejoicing in our early dawnings of light, we did not lift our eyes to.

But now there comes, as it were, another silent voice of God, saying, "Let there be a firmament." And God made the firmament and called it heaven. In other words, Let the regenerating man now see that he has a heavenly region or faculty of mind; let him perceive that he can withdraw himself from earth and earthly things and dwell in those above; let him realize that he is of a double nature and is possessed of a double mind, one degree of which is for the performance of his allotted part on earth, the other for his preparation for heaven; one by means of which he earns his daily bread, the other, within whose quiet realms he communes with God; one which renders him a natural man for the world's natural work, the other which renders him a spiritual man, and an heir of an eternal kingdom, whose wisdom, love and happiness as far exceed the earthly as light exceeds darkness, as heaven exceeds earth.

When, in the parable, we read the expression, "And God said," we must not imagine that an audible Divine voice resounded through space, bearing those words through its vast immensity. We must avoid all literal ideas as we would successfully grasp the spiritual purport. The voice of

God is the Divine dictate to the heart. It is as silent as the sunbeam that commands verdure from the earth, bids the flower mantle itself in red or blue or gold, and says to the spreading branches of the tree, "Be laden with fruit." When, then, the earth is in a condition to receive and respond to the solar rays, it may be said to hear the commands of its golden monitor, the sun—to listen to his voice.

A poet, tracing the departure of winter, as winter is in more frozen climes than this, thus wrote:

> Spring came at last, with her vernal train
>   Of balmy breezes and rainbow showers;
> And the sun upsprung in the sky again,
> And looked upon earth which so long had lain
>   Denuded of verdure and flowers;
> And he said, O earth! be clothed once more—
>   O flowers! your bridal colors don,
> And lo, as he spake, from shore to shore,
> The earth was mantled in robes of green,
> And blossoms of every hue were seen,
>   Called forth by the voice of the sun.

The poets see these things in clearer light than do the theologians. It is because they frequently use the figures of the Bible. The voice of the sun that bids the earth rejoice they know to be a very silent one. It consists of solar power working in realms ready to respond to its voiceful influence.

So when the heart is open to Divine influences, they silently steal in and warm it up to a livelier appreciation of the beautiful and good; and a sense of yearning for something better than all this selfish toil and trouble thrills through its every energy, and a ray of light flashes through the mind giving it to comprehend somewhat of those better things and that better way for which the heart has yearned. It is the voice of God. No sound is heard. It is recognized only in the form of a gentle influence, whose Divine forces would lead us to things above our place of standing.

We shall have occasion, in our consideration of this history of the Creation, to read this expression quite often —"And God said," so let us be sure that we understand it well. Its meaning in every instance is, "There was a dictate of God to the heart."

So also when the parable giving forth the voice of God, says, "Let there be!" it means, "Let there be developed," or Let it come to the consciousness of the regenerating individual. And when it says, "And God so made it," it means, "And God so developed it or brought it to his consciousness." So the creation of the firmament which God is said to have made, is, from the spiritual idea, the bringing to man's consciousness the fact that there is a firmament, a heaven, a higher region of the mind, an elevated faculty of living and doing, which is above earthly thoughts and its vanities, earthly love and its stains, and earthly life and its delusions. This opening of the spiritual mind constitutes the essential feature of the second stage of regeneration.

I speak of the opening of the spiritual mind, or the bringing to our consciousness the truth that we possess such a faculty. Do not let us leave this expression involved in mystery. I use it in the same manner that I would speak of any other faculty.

The child is born with full capabilities and possibilities, and these in great variety, limited only to the peculiarities of his genius. These are to be opened, strengthened and developed. It is the object for which he is brought into existence. And this opening and development is by and through his surroundings as assisting means. Thus, he is born with the possibilities of walking and talking. But the power of using the tongue, lips and palate in the formation of words comes through the slow strengthening and development of the muscles of those organs by the constant effort to use them in speech. Parallel with this, the powers of the mind unfold to a sufficient extent to attach rational meanings to words, as fast as the ability to form them proceeds. Thus also the power of walking comes from incipient possibilities opened and developed into actual realities, by gradually through the use of the limbs gaining strength, and by slowly unfolding the facility of equilibrium, or of being able to balance the body without effort. All the possibilities of physical power exist in the infant. All the muscles, nerves, tendons, or whatever may be necessary, are there, only they are undeveloped as yet. They need but to be unfolded and strengthened in order to the full attainment and possession of all their great possibilities and uses. And just so it is with the mental or intellectual faculties. The imitative, comparing and reasoning powers, as yet only in embryo in the child, come forth by gradual unfoldings to their fullest fruitions. And they develop in infinite variety according to the differing forms of education with different individuals, or in harmony with their varying kinds of genius. In one the mechanical faculties become prominent; in another the mathematical; in others the mercantile, the artistic, the political, the musical, the poetical, the linguistic, and so on in endless variety. They all exist at birth in different degrees of possibility, according to the peculiar genius of the individual; they only need opening and developing.

These, however, are of the natural mind. But there exists a still higher range of faculties—the spiritual. They are, as we might say, distinctly above the others, as those are above the merely physical. The natural mind may develop without limit on the range of its purely natural faculties.

One after another of them may be opened and developed, and the individual enter into large possession of their wonderful powers, and yet have no spiritual capacity. A prize fighter may strengthen his physical powers to a marvelous degree and yet possess little intellectual development. The merely natural man may be intellectual in every worldly sense—a keen reasoner, an apt logician, a profound student, a mechanic, a poet, an artist, a musician—and yet be utterly unable to grasp a spiritual truth. His spiritual mind is unopened, or, if partially opened, undeveloped. It is, therefore, utterly impossible to cause any one to see a spiritual truth, or to understand the difference between a spiritual life and a merely natural one, whose spiritual faculties are unawakened, unopened, unstrengthened, or undeveloped.

But the more they are opened the further they can see in this regard; while the less they are opened the less they can see. The spiritual possibilities are born with every one. The spiritual mind, in its rudiments at least, exists with all, just as certainly as does the natural. It is as certain that one may become spiritually intelligent and living, as that he may walk and talk or as that he may learn, on the natural plane of things, to imitate, reason and compare. Yes, it is precisely as Paul says: "The natural man (that is, the natural mind), receiveth not the things of the Spirit of God; for they are foolishness unto him; neither can he know them, because they are spiritually discerned." How can one understand spiritual things when the spiritual mind or faculty has not been as yet developed?

Well, in this beautiful parable of the Creation— this history of the gradual unfolding of the spiritual nature, the creation or development of the firmament sets forth the development of the spiritual mind. It is evidently an all-important stage in the process of regeneration; for as there can be no physical strength until the muscle is developed, and no rationality until the rational mind is unfolded, what can there be of spiritual thought, discernment or love until the spiritual mind is opened?

Waters, as we learned in the previous discourse, are symbols of truths. The living waters which our Lord offered to the Samaritan woman was the living truth He came to deliver to a fallen world. The water to which reference is made in Isaiah where it is said, "With joy shall ye draw water from the wells of salvation," was the spiritual truth which our Lord, when he came, would teach them to draw from the Word of God. The river of water of life, which was seen by John, in his vision of the holy Jerusalem, to proceed from the throne of God, and which watered the tree of life, was a spiritual figure of truth as coming from the Lord to man, and nourishing within his heart that tree of life which is the love of God. And so it goes on through the entire Scripture. Waters correspond to the eternal truths of God.

As the firmament signifies the spiritual mind, what is *under* the firmament means all that is beneath the spiritual; in other words, that is worldly and natural. The waters under the firmament, then, are holy truths as they exist in the external or natural mind; the waters above the firmament are the same truths as they exist in the spiritual or internal mind. From early childhood on we learn truths concerning heaven and eternal life. Amid our worst surroundings we get them somehow or in some way. Amid better surroundings we learn of them even by the common conversation of playmates. We hear of God as the Maker of all things, and of heaven as the place where we go if we are good. We learn of the sacredness of the Sabbath. If we go to Sunday-school or if we have God-fearing parents, we are taught much more than this, besides little prayers, Scripture texts and Bible stories; and the sacred influences of church worship cling to us ever closely. All we thus learn goes at least into the memory, even though it affects us but little, even though when we come to adult age, we care little for it, or worse yet, are skeptical with regard to it. These truths have become implanted in the natural mind and memory, and do as we will, or think with reference to them what we may, they cannot be wiped out. They are the waters under the firmament.

But when we come to perceive the difference between the spiritual and the natural; when we come to recognize our ability to view things spiritually and from a spiritual standpoint, then these truths, which before were matters of memory and not of life, names without understood qualities, sentences with no adhering meaning—then these truths become living, glowing verities to us.

The fog when it rests upon the earth has little effect upon the growth of its wheat fields and gardens, but let it rise into the canopy above, gather into cloud, and drop in the form of rain, and all earth springs at once into new beauty and bloom. So the Lord's truths when held in its embrace by the natural mind are mere words and forms of expression, from whence no spiritual growth proceeds. But let them be elevated into the spiritual mind, where they are spiritually received, understood and rejoiced in, and they give the eternal freshness of spring to life in all its varieties and degrees, from the spiritual above to the earthly below.

So when we can see the difference between religious truths as mere words and statements, and the same truths as a realized joy; between the truths of God as lifeless forms of expression and the same truths as the sweet refreshment of the inner life, then a division has been made for us between the waters which are under the firmament and those which are above the firmament, and the second stage of regeneration becomes for us a pronounced reality.

It is from evening to morning again; from a state of comparative spiritual twilight to one of new dawning brightness. Always from evening to morning! How much more lovely than to have it from morning to evening! In that case our movement would be from light into obscurity. But the regenerative progress is always from comparative obscurity into comparative light.

So the Lord has given us the light which revealed to us the superiority of spiritual things. That was our first step. Now He has opened to our consciousness and our enjoyment the internal or spiritual mind—that degree or faculty which can grasp and enjoy spiritual ideas. And he has also rendered clear to us the distinction between natural views of things and spiritual; that is, between life and truth as the natural mind views them and the same as seen by the spiritual mind. This is the second step. Here, in the firmament above, in the spiritual man, is where we build our heaven. Earth in itself, earthly thought and earthly love, is no heaven. God does not call it so. But when the mind's firmament, its realm of spiritual thought, is opened to our consciousness, that becomes our heaven of retreat from all that is gross and sensual, from evil and from sin, from disorder, confusion and unrest, and there we can make our preparations for a higher ascent still on the ever upward-sloping path of regeneration.

III.

THE FIRST FRUITS OF SPIRITUAL LIFE.

And God said, Let the waters under the heavens be gathered together in one place, and let the dry land appear; and it was so. And God called the dry land Earth: and the gathering together of the waters called He Seas: and God saw that it was good. And God said, Let the earth bring forth grass, the herb yielding seed, and the fruit tree yielding fruit after his kind, whose seed is in itself upon the earth: and it was so. And the earth brought forth grass, and herb yielding seed after his kind, and the tree yielding fruit, whose seed was in itself after his kind; and God saw that it was good. And the evening and the morning were the third day.
—Gen. 1: 9-13.

For our natural education we look to parents and teachers, for our spiritual education we go to the Lord. Instruction concerning natural things we draw from text books supplied by human learning, but spiritual instruction is obtained only from that book of Divine revelation which we are accustomed to call the Bible. It is a mistake to look for religion in a work purely scientific which has been wrought out by natural observation and deduction; but it is an error much more serious to seek for natural learning in a volume that has been revealed by the Lord for spiritual purposes alone. In the one case we simply go for information to an incompetent authority, but in the other we are belittling the Word of

God in ascribing to it a character no higher than that which is possessed by the words of men. If the Bible has any purpose at all it is one that is spiritual. If it has an educational mission of any kind, it is one that is religious. If it is the Word of God, we are to look for this spiritual element in all its parts —in every chapter, verse and line.

The purpose of the Lord in inspiring the first chapter of Genesis was to give an account of the general principles according to which the regeneration of the human mind proceeds. By regeneration we mean that new birth of the soul which is its development from a merely natural, into a lofty spiritual condition—that gradual putting away of its selfishness and worldliness which gives it a higher, nobler and purer nature in accordance with the ideals set up by our Lord. The Scripture treats of this, in some manner, in all its parts. Where the lesson is not obvious on the surface it lies concealed within the narrative; and thus the letter becomes a parable of higher truth.

Upon this principle the first chapter of Genesis also is found to treat concerning spiritual things. It matters not that the surface appearance may be otherwise, a close analysis reveals that fact. Under the similitude of earth's creation is unfolded the progressive order in which the development of the spiritual nature of each of us all goes on—the successive steps by which we proceed forward to the realization of our highest possibilities. The biblical account of the creation is then a parable of the regeneration of the human mind and heart. It is written according to the universal method of Divine narrative, that is to say, by the law of correspondence or sacred symbolism. These things were dwelt upon at length in the preceding discourses of this series: here we can do little more than allude to them.

I will repeat also in very brief form the significance of the narrative as thus far considered. I do this both for the information of those who were not present on the two previous evenings, and for the sake of keeping up the connection of ideas with those who were.

The earth is a symbol of the human mind. It is so used by the Lord, both here and elsewhere, because of the beautiful correspondence between the earth as the germinating receptacle of seed and the mind as the fertile soil wherein the truths of God are sown. The earth brings forth vegetation of every kind, which proceeds from the first tender signs of life to blade, stalk, leaf, tree, flower and fruit. In like manner, the mind, having received and nurtured the seeds of spiritual knowledge, brings them forth. Its mental germinations are first of the memory, then of reflection, then of reason, then of love, until the full fruits of a rich spiritual life are brought to maturity.

The Sacred Scripture makes use of this symbol in all its parts. When the Psalmist exclaims to the Lord, "All the *earth* shall worship thee, and shall sing unto thee," it is meant that all the minds shall so worship and sing. When he says that "the *earth* shall be full of the knowledge of the Lord," he means that the minds of his people shall be filled with that knowledge. And so our Lord, in teaching that regeneration, or the development of the mind on spiritual lines, is a gradual work, calls the mind of man the *earth* "which bringeth forth fruit; first the blade, then the ear, then the full corn in the ear."

The symbol as used in Genesis is the same. The *creation* of the *earth* is a parable of the *regeneration* of the *mind*. At first—so the narrative reads—the earth is a mere voidness and emptiness, and darkness is on the face of the deep; that is, the mind of man, before regeneration begins, is formless and void as to genuine goodness and truth, and the darkness of ignorance in reference to spiritual things rests upon its deeps.

As the great feature of the first day of creation was the fiat of God—"Let there be light!" so the main feature of the first stage of regeneration is the dispersion of the mind's ignorance and its obtainment of somewhat of light. The first dawn of light would consist, perhaps, only of an acknowledgment of the Lord and of the superior nature of spiritual things as compared with those which are merely natural. As without light earth could not have progressed into a condition where vegetation were possible, so without an acknowledgment of the Lord and of the superiority of heavenly things to worldly—without some light upon spiritual subjects, there can be no growth of the higher mind, no developments into nobler life, no flowers of the soul, no fruits of a religious spirit.

And as the great feature of the second day of creation was the development of the firmament of heaven, and the division of the waters which were under the firmament from those which were above; so the essential feature of the second state of the progress of the regenerating person is the opening of the firmament of the mind—its higher realm—its spiritual degree or faculty, whereby it is able to know, think and converse intelligently about spiritual things. The firmament of the narrative was called heaven; the mind's firmament is the region where heavenly thoughts prevail. Waters we found to be symbols of truths. The Divine truth presents itself in the beginning of this narrative in two symbolic aspects—as light and as water. Light symbolizes truth as illuminating the mind; water symbolizes truth as bedewing, fertilizing and refreshing the mind. The waters under the firmament of heaven are truths concerning spiritual things as they are held by the natural mind, beneath the arena of spiritual comprehension, heard perhaps, remembered as forms of words or unheeded expressions, scripture sentences even, carefully stored away in the memory, but under, not elevated into the firmament or heaven of the mind's spiritual degree. The waters above the firmament are the same truths elevated into spiritual apprehension—lifted up into that region of the mind which discerns spiritual things. It is there that the distinction between what is natural and what is spiritual begins to be seen. It is there that the division of the waters takes place.

The first state of regeneration, therefore, as symbolized by the first day of creation, is light let in upon the mind as to the superiority of spiritual knowledge and life over natural; the second is the opening of the spiritual mind, or of the faculty which discerns things spiritually.

Clearly, so long as one refuses to recognize at all the beauty of spiritual knowledge or life, he cannot enter upon the regeneration. When he does this he can make no further progress until his power of understanding spiritual truth is developed. For then first he is able to see the distinction between his spiritual mind or nature and his natural, between love of self and the world and love of God and man, between essential evil and essential good. Well settled preliminaries are necessary to progress. So soon as one can make these distinctions, and not before, he is ready to proceed further.

Let us now pass on to a consideration of the third state or stage of regeneration as set forth in the sacred symbols of the narrative.

"And God said, Let the waters be gathered together in one place and let the dry land appear." The allusion here is not to the waters above the firmament, but to those beneath. Waters, as we have seen, signify divine truth. The waters under the firmament we have found to signify those truths as mere forms, expressions or remembered texts, not spiritually realized or understood.

It is easy for one to have a knowledge of what he does not understand. The blind man may know that there is such a thing as light, because he has often heard it spoken of. So many have spoken of it within his hearing that he even *believes* in its existence. But what does he understand or realize concerning it when he has never seen it? So, a child may be taught that there is a God. Perhaps he firmly believes it because he has been so often told so. But what does he comprehend concerning the infinite existence of God—his love, mercy, wis dom, majesty? What realization has he of the marvelous ways of God in the creation and preservation of all things, of his wondrous influence as a potential presence in the soul? And what can he really grasp concerning these things until his mind is developed into such a faculty of spiritual thought as enables him to realize something of the nature of God? Until then God is little more to him than a name. The child's first theological lesson is a *knowledge* of God, but the spiritual minded adult's matured idea is a comprehension of the truth. But knowledge usually precedes understanding, and is, therefore, good so far as it goes. Knowledge of spiritual things, however, is only of the natural mind. Realization of them is of the spiritual mind. Knowledge is only of the memory; understanding is a far higher faculty.

The waters under the heaven, then, symbolize the knowledge concerning God, heaven and eternal life, concerning goodness and love and the sacredness of spiritual things which we gain *as* knowledge merely. All the information concerning these things we gain in childhood is of this character. They are not realizations, they are not really things comprehended. They are believed only because our parents or teachers tell us so. And the same holds good with all truth of a religious character that we learn in after life, just so far as it has not entered the spiritual understanding.

But these waters are said to be gathered by the Lord into one place. This is an expression, in symbolic form, of the truth that what we learn of spiritual things is first gathered together in the memory. Leaving out of consideration the physical organs, the brain and its various parts, through which the intellect primarily operates, the mind itself has many organs. One of these, and perhaps, the lowest of these, is the memory. It is the *one place* into which all mental impressions are first gathered.

God creates everything well. All things are arranged by him in true order and with reference to what is yet to come. It is true of the physical universe and it is true of man as a material and mental being. Equally true is it of man as a spiritual being. Creation in all of its developments proceeds by orderly stages. Learning precedes understanding; memory precedes comprehension. The child, for instance, learns his figures and his multiplication table and various rules of arithmetic at first as mere things of the memory. It is only afterwards as he comes to make application of them to matters of practical import that he realizes the use and beauty of them, and understands why they were so given. First stored up in the memory as mere dead matters of knowledge, then they are elevated out of his memory and into the rationality as useful things of life. "Twice two is four" is a very queer and stupid piece of information as it falls first upon the ears of the youthful mind. But let him go to the shop and find out that the two sticks of candy he has bought at two cents apiece make four cents that he has to pay the shopkeeper, and quite a new light breaks in on his mind as to the meaning and value of that, to him, most mystic phrase. And as he grows up and enters into the business of life, and sees the wonderful uses of arithmetic in all their every day aspects and gets, almost without reflection, to see the reasons of its rules and combinations, arithmetic rises out of the memory into the understanding.

And in learning music, we are first taught, and we store up in the memory, all knowledges with regard to musical facts, terms and tones. We learn about the lines and spaces, the notes and staves, the tones and semi-tones, and a hundred other things, as dry as dry can be to the young mind, and they are all stored away in the memory. But when these are brought into practical application, and their uses are clearly seen, and it is realized so that nothing can be plainer, that there can be no making of music without these as the necessary elements; and when we sing beautiful songs and play delightful melodies by means of our knowledge of them, why then that knowledge has advanced into understanding, realization, joy of soul, by its practical adaptation to the uses for which it was designed. It may remain mere dry knowledge, and with many learners it does, but with those who come into full comprehension of its adaptability to the making of real music, by the practical application of its principles, it has been elevated out of the memory and into the understanding.

These may seem small matters to the thoughtless mind, but they are not. They are illustrations of a most important principle. Knowledge is one thing, understanding what we know is quite another. Knowledge is an exceedingly good thing as a stepping stone to understanding—a necessary thing indeed; but alone and by itself, and without its proper increment, its value is infinitely diminished.

But the importance of the principle and of these very homely illustrations of it lies in the fact that it is precisely so with all things of spiritual import. Stowing away in the memory outward statements of religious doctrine however true, formulas of faith, or scripture texts however well learned, is one thing. But to gain a true idea of them; to lift them out of the memory into spiritual understanding and realization; thus to see their beauty and feel their rationality, to hold them as the delight of the soul to have them sweeten the life, to bring their influences into practical bearing on every work and duty, to love the Lord and the neighbor with them, to rise into heaven by their means; why—this is quite another thing. But we must get knowledge before we can get understanding. We must store up what we learn in the memory before we can take it out and transfer it into ideas of use and beauty. It is on precisely the same principle that food must be gathered together in one place, the stomach, before it can be put to its proper use. There its life-giving essences are separated and preparations for their distribution made. Then they go forth through their proper channels to the making of blood, flesh, bone, muscle, nerve or brain, and contribute each moment to the constant re-creation of man's physical system. The memory is the store-house of the soul. Reflection gathers from it its food for thought. Reason selects from its treasures the best elements for the development of mind. Wisdom looks down into its treasury of facts and weaves from them a heavenly life.

So the waters under the heaven gathered together into one place are the knowledges of spiritual and Divine things which become stored in the memory. This storing of the mind is of the providence of the Lord. It is in the direct line of his way of doing things. He desires that the memory shall be so filled for the soul's future use. If the man is himself opposed to the study of spiritual things, he is providentially led amid such circumstances and surroundings, as, unconsciously to himself, secure in some degree, the desired end.

It is said, "Let the waters under the heaven be gathered together into one place, and *let the dry land appear.*" Here the natural thought at once reverts to the idea of a separation effected between the oceans and continents of earth. It is as though, whereas, all before was one vast sheet of circling water, the Lord now said, "Let the dry land arise above the waves." But the spiritual thought goes forth on different lines. A dry tree would be a dead tree. A perfectly dry physical human body would be a lifeless mummy. In the language of sacred symbolism that is called dry which is devoid of spiritual life. As earth or land signifies the mind, the dry land is the mind without spiritual life. When, therefore, in this parable of the creation, that is, of man's regeneration, the Lord exclaims, "Let the dry land appear," it is as though He had said, "Let now the regenerating man see how dry—how spiritually dead and lifeless is the land of his mind. Let its dryness appear to him."

There is no dryer task in life than that of pouring the waters of mere knowledge, of mere memorized facts, into the sandy plains of the memory. Every schoolboy knows that. It is only as he understands or usefully applies what he learns that it becomes interesting to him. Now the man, we assume, has been all his life, consciously or unconsciously gathering the dead knowledges of religious instruction into his memory. If he is a student of religious things he may fancy that this constitutes him a religious man. But it does not. If he is a worldly man he may fancy that the ideas of morality he has, and a vague belief in God and a future state, make him all right. He also is mistaken. The land of his memory, albeit it is of moral and spiritual truths, is as dry as his spiritual nature is lifeless. But now that he has reached the proper state for further advance, the Lord desires he should know how dry and lifeless these knowledges he has gained are. So he says in the parable, "Let the dry land appear!" "Let it appear to you how dry and lifeless the land of the memory in itself considered is."

"And God called the dry land earth." The names of things in Scripture are always indicative of their quality. This expression is, in the peculiar form of ancient sacred symbolism, simply a statement that the earth or land of the mind is at this period of regeneration still spiritually dry and barren. When it is said God calls a thing so, it means that in the view of the Lord so and so it is.

"And the gathering together of the waters called He seas." This is so stated because as the sea is an aggregation of many streams of water, the memory is an aggregation of many streams of knowledge. Therefore, as the gathering together of the waters means the collecting of truths in the memory, seas are used throughout the Scripture to signify the memory as the first great receptacle of spiritual knowledges in their various degrees and kinds.

"And God saw that it was good," Everything in its order and degree is good in the sight of God. It is good that the law of order should be followed. It is good that regeneration should progress in an orderly way. It is good to gain the knowledges, facts or truths with regard to the Lord, a spiritual world, a spiritual life and other spiritual things, so as to store them away in the memory. That is, it is good, if it leads on to the higher life for which only they are useful.

"And God said, Let the earth bring forth grass, and the herb yielding seed, and the fruit tree yielding fruit after his kind, whose seed is in itself upon the earth." Here we have the similitude which tells of the mind actually yielding its first fruits of spiritual life. The object of all religious knowledge is religious life. It is utterly useless to know of the higher things of the Lord and not to love them. Indeed all knowledge is worthless unless it is applied to use. But to know God and not to attempt to do his will, to know what the life of love is and to live in an utterly selfish manner, to understand the nature of heaven and to live by merely worldly rules is a miserable squandering of the gifts of God. Unless at least a genuine effort is made to bring that knowledge forth into every day life, the gaining of it will prove to be a matter of very little consequence. The faculty of knowledge has been conferred upon us in order that we may put to its highest use the knowledge that we gain. When, therefore, dawning light breaks in upon us as to the greater value of that which is spiritual, and the higher mind is so opened that we can make clear distinctions between what is spiritual and what is natural in knowledge, thought, love or life, then we are to live in the light we have gained. This beginning to live it is the third stage of regeneration.

At the outset our efforts will be feeble and their results small. They will be more like those first efforts of young eaglets to fly, which consist in trying their wings only to see what they can do, than like the flights of conscious strength they make when fearlessly soaring above the mountain tops.

The idea that we can come into full spiritual strength and life in a single moment by a miraculous exercise of the grace of God, though widely entertained, is contradicted by all that our Lord has ever taught. In his parabolic method of speaking, it is always first the blade, then the ear, then the full corn in the ear; it is first the seed, smallest of all seeds, then the herb, then the tree. These illustrations of his are designed to teach the direct truth of progressive regenerative growth. One might as well undertake to ascend a mountain without taking the necessary series of upward successive steps, or from a child to become an adult by an instantaneous effort, as to become regenerated without passing through, and slowly through, the proper successive stages of progress. So none may feel discouragement because they do not come into all truth at once, or lose their many evils, sins and faults at once, or gain the perfect love for God and man at once.

There is very little real good in our first upward efforts—very little of the Lord in them. In whatever of good we seem to do we, in heart, take the credit to ourselves. Thus there is little genuine humility in our religion. It is the easiest thing in the world to imagine we are humble when, really, we are proud. People are sometimes proud of their humility.

As a matter of truth the Lord alone regenerates us. It is He only who infuses the good into our desires, thoughts or acts. Our part is simply to yield to those influences. Then under their impulse we, in the freedom with which we are endowed, endeavor to avoid what is wrong in purpose, thought or deed. But, in our first beginnings to fly, like the young birds, we come to the ground very often. We do it especially in this, that we deem whatever of spiritual progress we make to be so made in our own strength. In this position of mind the Lord gets but little of the credit. We may, indeed, *say* that it is the Lord's influence, aid and strength; but we do not feel it, do not realize his presence as in the effort, do not from our real hearts so acknowledge it. We imagine we acknowledge things sometimes when we really do not. And one of the most common perversities of human nature is for a man to think he believes a certain thing, when underneath and behind his thought, concealed from his own immediate view, is a huge distrust of the very truth that he *thinks* he thinks.

Yet notwithstanding the small amount of spiritual life which is to be found in these first efforts at living out so much of the truth of God as we have begun to profess, this third state of regeneration is a most valuable experience. The swimmer would never have learned to swim unless he had made his first floundering exertions. Milton would never have penned his immortal poem if he had not made his first poor attempt at writing verse. And the fact that he might have deemed his first efforts at versification very exquisite when they were quite the contrary, does not in the least detract from their value as beginnings. The Lord never despises beginnings. But He puts them at their true worth, and values them only *as* beginnings.

Therefore, in this account of creation as a parable of regeneration, what the mind brings forth is still expressed under the similitude of what the earth brings forth. This third stage of regeneration is described by the springing forth of vegetation, first, in its lower forms of grass, then in the higher forms of the herb yielding seed, and at last in the highest form of the fruit tree yielding fruit. Thus you will observe that on the third day of creation the earth brings forth something that has life. The lesson of the similitude is that in the third stage of regeneration the mind develops somewhat of spiritual life. Let us see this in the proper order of the words of the parable.

"And God said, Let the earth bring forth grass, and the herb yielding seed, and the fruit tree yielding fruit after his kind, whose seed is in itself upon the earth." The earth is the mind. The grass or low growth of vegetation which it brings forth symbolizes the first germinations of really *spiritual* endeavor, put forth by the mind. The herb yielding seed is a higher form of vegetation. It refers, naturally, to the various grains, such as wheat, barley, or rye, whose seed is a nutritious food for man. But spiritually it is a higher spiritual endeavor which produces something true and good. The fruit tree yielding fruit represents a still higher endeavor which bears the fruits of a yet more spiritual life. The idea is still enforced in the parable that even first endeavors at spiritual things have their degrees of effort, weak, stronger, stronger yet, good, better, better still, as life goes on.

It is said, "Whose seed is in itself upon the earth," in allusion to the natural fact of the tree producing fruit in which is seed and from whence new trees spring forth to the production of still other fruit, again producing seed, and thus, as it were, in a circle perpetually. The spiritual truth this represents is, that what is spiritual tends to produce continually newer forms of spiritual thought and life and this in endless succession forever.

"And God saw that it was good." Yes, God sees that this also is good; good again, however, for its time and season; good as a stepping stone to the better. For that which is yet more spiritual must, in its due order, come.

Vegetable life, it must be remembered, is after all and at its best, the lowest form of life. When we say of a man that "He does not really live, he only vegetates," we use a proverbial form of expression that conveys no very high opinion of the man. There are three orders of natural life, the vegetable, the animal and man. They are each excellent in their order and degree. But man alone has rationality and speech. Beasts have instinct only. Vegetation, no conscious existence at all. But vegetation, when the three are symbolically compared, typifies only the first and lower germinations of spiritual endeavor and life, upon which the higher principles when they come into development will, as it were, feed.

Our spiritual life, such as it is, in this third stage of regeneration, is not a conscious spiritual life. We make endeavors, we live in a more orderly manner, we break fewer commandments, but we have no conscious life of the Lord in mind or heart. The highest type of spiritual man realizes the Divine presence in the soul; he feels that he lives from it; he basks it in its sunlight. Just what this means we will see further on in our consideration of the parable of creation. But he who is only beginning this better life feels his efforts as his own. He may indeed with his lips acknowledge the Lord in them, but he has no inward realization of what that means, no consciousness of the Divine presence. It is right that it should be so. Beginnings are only beginnings, and the Lord sees that it is good; good, however, in its degree, no further.

So in this stage of regeneration the earth is only yielding its first fruits, not its best. On this plane of life, though good as compared with the old voidness and darkness, we are, spiritually speaking, only vegetating after all. We have had our evening of darker state and we stand in the morning of one better than the last. The evening and the morning are indeed the third day, but if we turn not back the revolving wheel of our re-creation there are four more yet to come. All in its time and order. Although we are but vegetating there is no cause for discouragement. We cannot go higher unless we stand on what is lower and take our upward step from thence; and everything, however imperfect as being comparatively low, is good as a standing place from whence to mount to things above.

And so we come to this point and the work still goes on. We stand among the sheaves of our garnered grain; we taste the rich fruits of a better life than once we had even dreamed of; but we look earnestly forward, lovingly higher, and wonder what better things the Lord has yet in store for us, in states of regenerative experience of which we have dim visions but have not reached as yet.

And so we see how beautifully the parable of the creation, when viewed in its inward meaning, sets forth the regeneration of the human soul. In the very consideration of its symbols, and in the explanations and illustrations which necessarily connect themselves therewith, we are developing the true philosophy of the spiritual new birth, and are learning to place that most interesting subject on its true basis. We are gaining, not human opinions which may or may not be true, but the absolute inwardness of revelations, which, because they are divine, are truth itself.

IV.

THE ELEVATION OF LOVE AND FAITH.

And God said, Let there be lights in the firmament of the heaven to divide the day from the night; and let them be for signs, and for seasons, and for days, and years; and let them be for lights in the firmament of heaven to give light upon the earth; and it was so. And God made two great lights; the greater light to rule the day, and the lesser light to rule the night; he made the stars also. And God set them in the firmament of heaven to give light upon the earth, and to rule over the day and over the night, and to divide the light from the darkness; and God saw that it was good. And the evening and the morning were the fourth day.—Gen. 1 : 14-19.

In three previous discourses we have considered the subject of the first three days of creation. We have thus learned for what the Biblical narrative of that event was not designed and for what it was. Thus, it was not designed to be an account of the literal creation of the earth; it was not intended as a lesson in cosmogony or geology or any other branch of natural science. But it had, of course, a Divine purpose and meaning. This purpose was to set forth in parable or sacred allegory a series of spiritual truths.

The seven days of creation were thus found to symbolize the seven stages of progress through which man passes in the regeneration. He is born merely natural and at first develops only his natural powers and mind. But it is also designed by his Creator that he shall become spiritual and develop his spiritual powers and mind. This development, always gradual and slow, is called in Scripture the regeneration.

At first, and before regeneration begins, we are in ignorance, or, at least, in non-acknowledgment of spiritual things. A little child knows nothing as to its spiritual nature. It may *learn* a little with regard to it, but what it learns it does not really understand. The adult, who takes no interest in anything but his worldly affairs and pleasures, and does not see anything in a spiritual idea when it is presented to him, has not gone many steps, in this, beyond the child. His mind may have developed largely on natural lines, but certainly not on spiritual. As, however, he takes more interest in things of higher import, and comes more and more under their influence, he makes steps of progress herein. This progress in the unfolding of the higher elements of his being is his regeneration. And as the Biblical narrative of the creation sets forth under the form of parable, and in the language of sacred symbolism, the history of man's regeneration, the seven days in which the progressive events of the earth's creation are related, symbolize the seven general states of progress through which all have to pass from the merely natural to the higher spiritual.

Your minds were then directed to the truth concerning the particular ideas involved in the statements with reference to the first three days. I called your attention to the fact that the earth was, throughout the Scripture, a symbol of the mind of man. The condition in which it was previous to creation, its being without form and void, was a perfect illustration of the state of each one's mind previous to regeneration. As to religious ideas or purposes, it is without form and void. The darkness which was said to dwell, at that time, on the face of the deep, symbolized the great darkness as to spiritual things, which is the first condition of all, previous to their entrance upon the regeneration. Ignorance, as to this phase of knowledge, life and power, broods upon the face of their mental deeps.

If one is in ignorance, or in non-acknowledgment of the truth of any subject, the first step is to get light upon it, to gain information concerning it, and *such* information, and in such form, that he may be able to see and believe it. The first light on spiritual subjects is that whereby we acknowledge its primary principles, such as, that there is a God and that spiritual things are, in themselves, of a higher nature and of more importance than worldly things.

This, as we learned, was represented in the parable by the command of God, "Let there be light," and its resulting consequence, "there was light." And this, the first day of creation, symbolizes the first stage of regeneration—some light let in upon the darkness of the mind.

Having gained this much, the second step is to acquire a habit of understanding spiritual truth when it is presented to the mind; in other words, to have the spiritual understanding opened or the spiritual mind developed. This, we found to be represented by the creation of the firmament. The natural firmament or sky is the region above, through which light irradiates the realms of space and pours in upon the earth. Correspondingly the spiritual firmament of the mind is where light on spiritual themes is received and spread around, and into all the various faculties.

Having now obtained a mental power of receiving the Lord's spiritual teachings, and of comprehending them, the third step is the bringing forth of that which we have thus far gained into fruits of a good life. The prominent feature of the third day of creation was the earth bringing forth grass and the herb yielding seed and the fruit tree yielding fruit. These, being the first springings forth of life on earth, we found to be symbolic of the mind's first effort to bring forth into life something living and spiritual. It is vegetable life; it is not of a very high kind; still, it is life. So the covering of the field of the mind with the tender verdure of incipient spiritual resolves is represented by the Lord's clothing the earth with grass. The growth of the mind into the bringing forth of the fruits of good efforts, based upon what we have thus far spiritually understood, is figuratively delineated by the Lord causing the herb yielding seed and the fruit tree yielding fruit to spring up upon the earth.

And thus we gained and explained the meaning of the first three days of creation as symbolizing the first three stages of regeneration. In the beginning of earth's creation there was chaos and darkness. Then there was brought into being—on the first day, light; on the second, the firmament; on the third, vegetable life—grass, herbs, fruit. Observe the parallel. Previous to regeneration, in the case of every person, there is ignorance or denial— spiritual darkness. The first stage or progress consists in light—mental light concerning the superior value of spiritual things. The second is in the opening of the firmament of the mind, its upper realm of the spiritual understanding. The third is in the bringing forth of the first germinations of spiritual life and the first ripened fruits of higher principles.

Thus far we have proceeded, in our previous lectures, in the elucidation of this parable of the creation. We come now to the fourth day. This symbolizes the fourth stage of regeneration.

"And God said, Let there be lights in the firmament of the heaven to divide the day from the night; and let them be for signs, and for seasons, and for days and years; and let them be for lights in the firmament of the heaven to give light upon the earth; and it was so. And God made two great lights; the greater light to rule the day, and the lesser light to rule the night; he made the stars also. And God set them in the firmament of heaven to give light upon the earth, and to rule over the day and over the night, and to divide the light from the darkness."

These great lights, the greater light to rule the day, and the lesser light to rule the night, are, of course, the sun and moon. But there is a curious feature of this portion of the narrative to which the opponents of the Bible have not neglected to call attention. It is that the sun was not created until the fourth day. Now the sun is the well-known source of all our light. The moon only shines with the borrowed light of the sun. It is the sun which divides the day from the night—light from darkness. Its presence constitutes light and day; its absence is darkness and night. Yet the first act of the first day of creation was the fiat of God, "Let there be light," and the very first result of creative energy consisted in the fact that "there was light." Now, here is the paradox. The sun is the only source of natural light; the sun was not created until the fourth day; and yet there was light on the first day. The opponents of Bible-inspiration, therefore, put to us several very pertinent questions. If the sun was not created until the fourth day, how could there have been light on the first day? If light was created on the first day which divided the day from the night, the light from the darkness, what necessity was there for the creation of a new source of light on the fourth day for the purpose of effecting the very thing which had already been done on the first day? Or if two natural sources of light were at that time created, how is it and when was it, that the one originally made was blotted out from the face of the heavens or destroyed?

This question, from a strictly literal point of view, has never been answered. It cannot be. The nearest approach to an answer that has ever been given is, that it is one of those mysteries of religion which must be received by faith even though it be contrary to reason.

The believer in the truth that this is a spiritual parable avoids this confusion. When he understands its meaning, he sees at a glance the figurative reasons for its taking that form. Knowing that it was given for the sake of its spiritual meaning only, he views the expressions as fully harmonious with that purpose. He may go even further and admit the force of a natural figurative meaning underlying the other which will harmonize these statements with the facts of known science. But the basic truth is that its primary form, force and meaning is spiritual.

And now let us see what the natural figures are that are here used, and what they spiritually mean.

On this fourth day there are lights set up in the firmament of heaven. They are placed there to give light upon the earth ; and to divide the day from the night, and to separate the light from the darkness. When we remember that the firmament of heaven typifies the spiritual mind, that is to say, the faculty of discerning spiritual things, the significance of these newly created objects becomes manifest. According to the laws of Divine symbolism, the sun is the symbol of love; the moon of faith, and the stars of knowledge. But as these are of little value except as they are directed to the Lord and derived from Him, the sun is frequently used to denote the Lord as the object of our love, the moon to denote the Lord as the object of our faith, and the stars to signify our knowledge concerning the Lord and his goodness and truths. Therefore we may say that the sun typifies the Lord as to love, and the moon the Lord as to faith; or we may say that the sun signifies love of the Lord, and the moon faith in the Lord. The meaning is the same. Love, in this its Divine sense, is always from the Lord and is the Lord in us. Faith is always given us by the Lord, and, in another sense, is the Lord in us. So whether we say, love, or love to the Lord, or the Lord as our love, it is, in its radical sense, about the same. Or whether we say, faith, or faith in the Lord, or the Lord as our faith, it is, virtually, the same.

The sun signifies the Lord because that solar orb rules in the realm of nature in a manner corresponding to that in which the Lord rules in the realm of spirit. It might be said that the sun of nature is the Lord's vice-gerent in the physical planetary spheres. As the sun gives heat and light to the world of nature, the Lord gives spiritual warmth which is love, and spiritual light which is understanding to the world of the mind. As the sun causes the earth to be covered with verdure, germinates the seed, swells the bud, develops the leaf and flower and fruit, and gives life, growth and renewal to all things, so the Lord causes the mind to become clothed with the verdure of spiritual life, brings forth with his gentle influences the blossoms and fruits of the spirit, fills with life its affections and thoughts, and gives strength and growth to its varied faculties. And could we but peer into the domain of the higher spheres of the world beyond, we would see the Lord as the beneficent sun or life-giver of its entire spiritual realms.

But the sun typifies the Lord as love, because it is the sun, in respect to its warmth, which makes the earth so full of life and beauty, as it is the Lord, in respect to his affectionate warmth of love, who renders living, glowing, real, all that fills the world of the mind. Our hearts warm toward what we love; they are cold toward what we love not. Love is the warmth of the spiritual nature. It is the Lord's gift of love which warms us toward Himself, toward religion, toward spiritual study, toward the higher life and work, just as it is the sun's heat which warms, revives and renovates the earth.

This symbol of the sun as representing the Lord, and especially the Lord as our love, is as old as human religion. It was the origin of sun-worship. For as the sun was first used as a symbol only of the Deity, and as such temples were adorned with its semblance and dedicated to its name, through the decadence of religion the symbol became, in human thought, the reality; and the sun, in its origin, the type of God, became to idolatrous nations the great God himself.

That the moon symbolizes the Lord as our faith may be illustrated by these considerations: The moon shines by reflected light, while the sun is light and heat in itself. The faith of the mind is true and bright only as it is reflected from love — only as it is a response to the deep love of the heart. The moon's light is borrowed from the sun. Sunlight, therefore, is the great natural power of life and growth which broods upon the face of the earth. Moonlight has very little to do with covering the land with corn, with filling the gardens with flowers, or with loading the trees with fruit. The moon without the sun would have neither light nor life. Faith without love is cold and dead. It can neither warm the heart, enlighten the mind, nor give salvation to the man. But faith that is kindled at the shrine of the heart's best love, faith which borrows its light from love, faith which reflects the sunny glow of the heart's true love on every pathway of life—that is at once the sign and seal of a soul that is saved.

Thus while the Lord lights up our life with love, when love is triumphant in the world of the heart, it is faith which lights the path when all is dark. When we are happy, when we are loving, when we are in states of elevated spiritual feeling. when it is *day time* for the soul, we feel, and see, and recognize the Lord as lighting with his love our world of life. I speak, of course, of those who *do* recognize God's providence as permeating all our ways. But when all is dark and hope is waning, and evils overflow our heart-land, and even *outward* life seems all unhinged—when it is *night time* on the soul, then the faith we have that God is true, the faith we hold in his mercy and love as things that never die, the faith we still maintain that the night will pass away and the day will come—that faith sustains us in adversity, in trial, in temptation, in doubt, yea raises us even from the depths of despair. Thus it is, that with him who has so far progressed on the upward way of regeneration, it is the sun, or love of God, which rules in the soul by day, but the moon, or faith in God, which rules therein by night.

That the stars symbolize knowledges of the Lord and of what is true and good may be illustrated by these considerations: In the absence of any correct understanding of things, a knowledge of its rules and principles light our way to some extent. As I have elsewhere remarked, knowledge is one thing, understanding what we know another, and a loving life of what we understand another still. We may have a knowledge of the customs of polite society. They are mere outward show, but, nevertheless, they smooth our path in the world. But if we understand the ethics of true kindliness and gentleness, we can take up the rules of outward etiquette, and make them beneficent methods of smoothing the rugged paths of others' lives. If, however, we love from our hearts to live and walk through life for the sake of strewing sunshine and flowers and deeds of use o'er all the paths which others tread, then the inward ethics of true heavenly etiquette intuitively come forth in every moment of our lives. So in matters which concern our spiritual walk, where neither love nor faith shine on our wandering way to guide our devious steps, the stars of the mere knowledge of what is true and good may afford some glimmering light to help us on. Thus, as in the absence of sun and moon, night may still have its stars, comparatively dim though their light may be, so, though our love may, for the time, be cold, and our faith may halt, the bare knowledge of what is true and good will serve a purpose in our lives, until our faith and love assert themselves once more.

When we read the Scripture by these symbols, so far as they therein occur, it confirms the truth of their symbolism, as well as throws light upon its otherwise darkened pages. It is said for example in the Psalm: "Praise ye the Lord, sun and moon; praise him all ye stars of light." Can any one believe that this is designed as a literal command to sun, moon and stars to enter upon intelligent praises of the Lord? Nay; the sun, moon and stars to whom appeal is thus made are set up in the firmament of the mind of man. It is a command to all mankind to let their love, their faith, their knowledges of God and good, go forth in the silent praise which the warmth, and light, and clear shining of a genuine spiritual life forever render to the Lord. When, amid the higher and holier states of life, the heart arises to the Lord with loving thanks, whether silent or expressed, when, amid its darker states of trial and temptation, in unbroken faith, it hopes and trusts in Him, when, in the momentary lull of either or of both, its knowledges of the true and good, of God and heaven, still assist in the dispersion of the gross darkness of merely natural life, then do the sun, moon and stars of the mind praise the Lord. Then is the command of the sacred psalm fulfilled.

In that oft-repeated prophecy of our Lord concerning his second coming, it is said, "The sun shall be darkened, and the moon shall not give her light, and the stars shall fall from heaven." Shall we then entertain so foolish an idea, as that the natural sunlight shall be obliterated; that the natural moon shall lose her power to shine; that the myriad of stars which stud the sky, many of them inconceivably larger than the earth on which we live, shall fall on this one small globe? The meaning is simply this: that in the days when our Lord should make his second coming, the sun would be darkened, in the sense that genuine love to the Lord would cease to radiate from the hearts of men; that the moon would not give her light, in the sense that true faith in Him would cease to shine within the souls of men; and that the stars would fall from heaven, in the sense that men's knowledges of spiritual things would fall from their high and heavenly hold upon the human mind, and become earthly, material and debased.

So the fourth day of creation, as the parable relates, was the setting up of the sun, moon and stars, to rule over the day and over the night. And the fourth stage of regeneration is when love to the Lord, faith in the Lord, and knowledges of the Lord's truths, are set up in the spiritual or internal mind to rule the whole realm of heart and mind, affection and thought.

Let us understand this fully. Shall we ask what love is? It is easy to *feel* what it is, but it is difficult to bring it within the scope of definition. Attachment, preference, liking, fondness, affection, are expressions of somewhat the same meaning, but they do not present the idea of vigor, warmth, depth or intensity which seems to attach to the term *love*. The word, in all its fullness of meaning, is absolutely without an equivalent in the language

It is positively incapable of definition. Yet if we have love toward others, we know how our hearts warm to them, how we long for their presence, how we are willing to drop all selfish considerations for their sakes, what sacrifices we are ready to make to render them happy, how willing we are to do and dare, to work, to surrender, to live for them. Love is gentle, kind, disinterested, diligent, constant, and these in all things, to the person loved. This, of course, is its highest type; but all not thoroughly brutalized have experienced it in some degree. One of the most tender types of this love is that of a mother to her child. One of the broadest is that of love of country, in whose behalf thousands have no hesitation in laying down their lives.

Let us now apply this to the Lord. Let us think of Him as the embodiment of all that is lovely and wise, of all that is true and good. In any such sense as we approach our earthly friends, we cannot see Him, we cannot hear Him, we cannot touch Him; nor can we have that kind of sense of personal devotion to Him which we have toward those who meet us on our own plane of life. But we can think of God as our glorified Christ; we can hold Him before our mental vision as an infinitely lovely Divine man; we can send our hearts forth to Him as the one good and true, from whom all that is good and true comes down.

And that is just the point. He stands as our highest conception of infinite goodness and truth— of infinite love and wisdom. He has given us his commands of perfect life. In these commands He has embodied in words the ideal to which He would have us attain—an ideal which is reflected from his own person and life. Now when we fall in love with that perfect ideal as personally represented in Him, and as expressed in the instructions He has given us in his Word, we have fallen in love with Him. We cannot separate our ideal from his person, because in Him alone that perfect life is perfectly revealed. If we drop his personality from thought in this connection, our ideal of perfection loses its glory or sinks into something less than perfect. It is only as we remember his description of a perfect life as embodied in his instructions, and apply them to Him, Jesus, our incarnate God, and observe in Him a complete realization of a completely sinless life, that we can fall in love with the absolutely true and good as He would have us do. No mere man can reflect to us that infinitely harmonious perfection which Jesus can.

We know God, we realize God, we think of God, we love God, only as He is revealed to us in Christ. Essential divinity, as it is in its own infinite being, the finite idea cannot grasp. We can grasp it only as it is brought down to our vision. We see God, therefore, ever, in thought, as Jesus glorified. With what is invisible, incomprehensible, unthinkable, we have, and can have, nothing, consciously, to do. The essential divinlty is more beyond us than your soul, which I can neither feel nor see, is beyond my ken. I know you only through your body, your speech, your outward life. You can know essential Divinity only as the soul of Christ—something entirely beyond and above your grasp. But *in* Christ, and through his life and speech and works, in that Humanity which was made Divine and now fills heaven and earth and all things, God becomes something which we can know of, think of, live for, love!

So we raise our hearts to this Divine Man. We see his life exemplified in the world; we hear the ringing precepts He uttered for our guidance of old and on earth; we love the good He lived, the truth He taught, the life He exemplified; thus, we love *Him*. So He himself has defined this love in the only way in which it can be defined, and He has said, "He that hath my commandments and doeth them, He it is that loveth me;"—"If ye love me, keep my commandments." And if we really love the life He offers for our acceptance, we *will* keep his commandments. If we do not, it is because we love ourselves, or the world's goods and pleasures better. But when we love them, or to the degree that we love them, what will we not do for the love of the true and the good, which is the love of God, which we would not do for a friend? Will not our hearts warm toward it? Will we not long for its presence within us? Will we not drop all selfish considerations for its sake? Will we not do all things, dare all things, surrender all things, to live for that, and that alone. While love for a friend will make us gentle, self-abnegating, watchful, diligent, on behalf of the person so loved; will not the love of the good and the true, for their own sakes and as exemplified by God on earth, make us all this and more, in all things, and toward all men? But whether we say the love of good, or the love of God, or the love of Christ, is it not all the same?

Now when this love begins to affect the soul, the greater light, of which our text speaks, is set up in the heaven, or spiritual region of the mind, to light our steps along all the pathways of life.

And what is faith? It is an internal belief in, or a certain conviction of the existence of, such a God, such a life, and such a love. A perfect faith has always understood, and, to a certain extent, realized that in which it believes. It cannot, therefore, be shaken. It believes in the goodness of God, in his mercy, his love and his providence, and, therefore, it sustains him who holds it amid the darkest episodes of life. Whether misfortunes come, whether temptations assail, whether doubts press in, in all these dark and troublous night-times of the soul, that unshaken belief in God as the only good, and in good as the only life, sustains our steps. Faith alone, faith which has not borrowed its light from love, cannot do this. But a faith that is the reflection of genuine love once ours, cannot by any possibility fail us.

So, when this belief in God which is born of love has power to sustain us amid our night-times of life, the lesser light, the moon of faith, begins to shine upon us with its silvery radiance. Set up within the spiritual region of the mind, it sheds light upon our darkness, illumines our farthest pathways, saves us from snares and pitfalls, and carries us safely on to another state of newly awakened day.

Then those beautiful knowledges of eternal things, in their vast variety, thoughts of God the Lord, conceptions of a true life, ideas of mercy, love and truth, far off glimmerings of a heaven beyond—all these shine down, help our faith to illuminate our mental world, maintain our light when faith itself is dim, but silently disappear to conscious view, when love irradiates the mind with so large a light and warmth, as to point the way to all things without manifest intellectual aid. Radiant stars on the mind's clear sky are they, whose lights reveal celestial mansions in the world to come. Knowledge may be ours and yet have no illuminating power. To learn eternal truths is one thing. They only become stars along our hastening way when they are kindled into fires in the firmament of the spiritual mind.

Knowledge is not faith; nor is faith, love. But without knowledge there can be no faith, and without both no love. Knowledge, faith *and* love are a trine of principles which in their blended lights dispel the last vestige of darkness from the mind.

So we have groped our way along, all in the providence of God, to our fourth state of regeneration. It is a slow process. We came out of darkness into light, but what did we realize of eternal things? We passed into a capacity for grasping spiritual thoughts, but what warmth or clearness was there to our new found views? We brought forth some fruits of a better outward life, but what was there in our works of genuine love? Or how clear a faith had we in the higher life of good, or the grander ways of God? But now this love and faith are enkindled within the spiritual mind, and even our knowledge of eternal things are lit with living fire.

And so these lights enkindled thus serve to divide between the day and night—between the light of the true and good and the darkness of the false and evil. Error can no more deceive us; evil can no more palm itself off for good, nor selfishness for virtue. These clear-shining luminaries, love, the greater light for the day, faith the lesser light for the night, have dispelled all misconceptions. And they serve for *signs* of our elevation and progress; they mark the *seasons* of our changing heart-conditions, and tell of the *days and years*—the ever-advancing states of truth and love. And they are set in the firmament of heaven—in the spiritual mind, to give light upon the earth, or illuminate its every lower place with spiritual radiance.

Then the previous state, when true love and genuine faith were not as yet possessed, is, as compared with the present state of love and faith, as evening shadow to morning light. And God sees that it is good. And the evening and the morning—this new advance from comparative obscurity into clearer light, are the fourth day—the fourth progressive state into which all who press on in the regenerate life will come.

Is life a mystery? Are its paths all darkness and unrest? Not to those who have made even the beginnings of a life of love and faith. Is there any light for the soul? Is there a way out of the shadows which obscure our wanderings? Yes; love throws a radiance over life which dispels all clouds; faith lights up its skies amid its gloomiest nights; true knowledge reveals bright homes in everlasting worlds beyond the one in which we linger now. And in that knowledge, faith and love the Lord lives and reigns supreme. Gain these and you have left the lower levels of a false life behind, and all things beckon you onward in your advancing way.

V.

THE SOUL BECOMES A LIVING THING.

And God said, Let the waters bring forth abundantly the moving creature that hath life, and fowl that may fly above the earth in the open firmament of heaven. And God created great whales, and every living creature that moveth, which the waters brought forth abundantly, after their kind, and every winged fowl after his kind; and God saw that it was good. And God blessed them, saying, Be fruitful, and multiply, and fill the waters in the seas, and let fowl multiply in the earth. And the evening and the morning were the fifth day.—Gen. 1: 20-23.

The subject of the regeneration is one of the utmost interest and importance. Our Lord said, "Except a man be born again, he cannot see the kingdom of God." Why should it not be so? The new-born babe is ushered on to its this-world existence a weak, unformed thing. Its body is formed, indeed, but not its mind. It has been born into the kingdom of nature; it has yet to be reborn and that into the kingdom of mind. When this takes place, and the once immature babe becomes a knowing, thinking and reasoning being, it has but partially fulfilled its destiny. It can live in this world, and use its knowledge of natural things with decision and skill; it has entered largely on to the realm of this world's thought; but it has again to be re-born. This time the birth is into the realm of spiritual thought. These things are progressive. There can be no rational, thinking being until the physical body is formed. There can be no spiritually minded being until thought and reason as natural things are developed. The one, in each case, constitutes a foundation, as it were, on which the other may rest.

Spiritual thought and natural thought, spiritual aspiration and natural aspiration, a spiritual life and a natural life, belong to distinctly different faculties of mind. After the natural mind is born and formed, the spiritual mind must be born and formed. This is the rebirth—the regeneration, of which our Lord spake, when He said "Except a man be born again, he cannot see the kingdom of God." To see the kingdom of God is to see spiritual things. It is to understand them when presented to the mind. It is to be able to revolve them rationally in the thought, to grasp them, to enjoy them, so as finally to come, in matters of every day life, into their living spirit and purpose.

But the kingdom of God extends into the hereafter as well as has its beginnings here. Our ability to enter upon its joys in the world to come depends upon the harmony of our minds with its principles, purposes and uses. It is not so much a question, when we arrive there, as to how much punishment ought to be meted out for our short-comings, or how much reward for our well-doing, as it is: Has the mind learned to see spiritual things—spiritual principles, ideas and uses, or has it not? Is the mind in harmony with the kingdom of God, or is it not? Has it entered into the spirit and purpose of that which essentially constitutes the heavenly kingdom, or has it not? You might as well ask the Hottentot, who has no musical development above his tom-tom, to enter into the refined enjoyment of the strains of Mendelsohn or Mozart, as to invite a merely natural or sensuous man, when he enters upon the other-world life to partake of the spiritual joys, associations, thoughts or uses of the heavenly kingdom. He would neither understand, appreciate or enjoy them. It is requisite that one should be born again to see the kingdom of God. Properly, this spiritual development should be made on earth. It is as much designed of God that the natural man should become a spiritual man, as it is that the physical babe should become a rational being.

If, then, it be true, that earth life is educational, looking to the preparation of the individual for the never-ending existence which awaits him in the world to come, it is the one great theme from which the mind should never be wholly averted. No one who leans in the least degree toward the doctrine of the superiority of spiritual things can doubt this.

As the regeneration of the soul is first in interest as it respects human welfare, it becomes, therefore, by right of priority, the first spiritual lesson we ought to learn. We would naturally expect to find a statement of its general phases, in the very opening chapter of the Word of God. In this, do we but view the matter aright, we will not be disappointed. The narrative of the Creation is but a parable of the regeneration. The earth is a symbol of the human mind. The statement that at the beginning all was dark and void, sets forth, in symbolic language, the mind's utter ignorance and emptiness of spiritual things before its regeneration begins. The fact that at the very outset of Creation light was flashed across the earth represents that at the very outset of regeneration, in the case of each one, light is thrown upon his mind as to the superiority of spiritual life and knowledge over that which is merely natural. The development of the firmament or natural heaven, typifies the opening of the higher or heavenly mind of spiritual observation and thought. The springing forth of grass and the growth of the fruit tree yielding fruit denote the first buddings and incipient fruitage of a good life under the more elevated principles now recognized. The setting up of the sun, moon and stars in the firmament of heaven symbolizes the elevation of love, faith and spiritual knowledge as the guiding and controlling elements of the regenerating individual's life.

The regeneration of the human mind is, therefore, progressive. It proceeds, as Creation proceeded, by distinct steps. The four days of Creation symbolize four successive stages of regenerative advance. First, some higher spiritual light was thrown upon the mind; second, the spiritual mind, or the faculty for the perception of spiritual things, was developed; third, good actions and a better life resulted; fourth, love, faith and knowledge, like great lights and stars of brilliant shining, lit up the life with their beautiful radiance. All this has been fully illustrated and explained in previous lectures. We now come to the fifth state of regeneration represented by the fifth day of Creation. In this state the man's spiritual condition begins, at last, to exhibit signs of genuine life.

But was not the individual really alive before? Naturally speaking, yes; spiritually speaking, no. In all the business, work, pleasures, ambitions and aspirations of the world, yes; in the higher and more inward ends, desires and motives of life, no.

And what is it to be alive? We ask this question, of course, in a sense above that which attaches to the idea of merely physical life. There is a phrase much affected of late years which illustrates the point. We hear of live political parties—these are such as drop dead issues and deal vigorously with the living questions of the day; of live newspapers—these are such as are enterprising in gathering all the news that interests, and in a racy handling of the topics of the times; of live men—these are energetic, earnest, pushing people, who rest not until they accomplish, and that successfully, whatever ends they undertake. The expression has come down, in a reflected form, from the ancient language of symbolism, in which the Scriptures are written. Only, in them the phrase is always spiritually applied.

There, *living* things are such as are touched by the breath of God. Natural things are held to be, in themselves, dead. A dead man, in the light of the Word of God, is one who is given over to selfishness and worldliness. A live man is one who has dropped the old, dead issues of a merely natural life, and deals vigorously with the living issues which the spiritual condition of the world and his own soul presents. He is enterprising in gathering unto himself the living truths that relate to higher life. He is energetic, earnest, pushing, in all that relates to the regeneration of his own soul and the leading of the world on to higher levels. He is alive to everything of spiritual import and eternal issue, because his faith in the Lord is established, his love to the Lord has taken some absolute form, and his knowledge of spiritual things is becoming varied and extended. The sun of love and the moon of faith are set upon the firmament of his spiritual mind, and new stars of knowledge come brightly shining forth upon his intellectual horizon with every advancing state.

These terms *living* and *alive* come forth in their symbolic significance so plainly in the Scripture that there is no mistaking them. Thus the one Lord is there recognized as life itself and consequently the only source of life. This is true naturally and spiritually. Especially is it true that He is the only source of spiritual life, because that is the more real. Therefore, in the Word, the Lord is called the *living* God, Him that *liveth* forever. He is also called the Fountain of *Life*, and the Fountain of *Living* Waters. And heaven which is heaven only by virtue of its inhabitants receiving his life, is called in many places "the land of the *living*." The term *living* waters is often used to indicate those spiritual truths which lead to everlasting life. In this view our Lord said to the Samaritan woman, "If thou knewest who it is that saith to thee, Give me to drink; thou wouldest have asked of him, and he would have given thee *living* water." *Living* bread is the Lord's spiritual life received as the nourishment of the soul. Said He, "I am the *living* bread which came down from heaven; if any man eat of this bread he shall live forever." *Living* men are those who think and act under the influence of the genuine spirit of the Lord and his commandments. In this view the Apostle said, "Likewise reckon ye also yourselves to be dead indeed unto sin, but *alive* unto God through Jesus Christ our Lord."

I have been thus particular in indicating the genuine spiritual meaning of this term as used in the Scripture, because upon it hinges the signification of the description of the fifth stage of man's regeneration as contained in the parable of creation. So you will observe that while man may be naturally alive, and perform his natural duties with energy and enterprise, without a single spark of living fire from off the altar of God, he can be spiritually alive only as he lives in the love, faith and knowledge of God, and performs all duties, natural and spiritual, in their light and under their influence.

In the early stages of regeneration, we begin to do right, because we think we ought so to do, but we do not exactly do it from the living fire of God within the heart. We recognize the Lord; we study his commands; we try to be just to the neighbor and punctual to our religious duties. But we do not see them from love, nor do we much enter into the deep spirit of their meaning and practice. While we are perfectly willing to *say* that all our good is from the Lord, we *feel* it as our own. And while we are free to admit that our regeneration is the Lord's work upon the soul, we are in a strong sense of our own efforts to that end. So much so is this the case that our consciousness is, all the time, that it is our own work. At this stage of regeneration it necessarily must be so. And we also speak the language of self-conscious effort, because in that state a higher language would almost savor of hypocrisy. We feel, therefore, our good as our own effort, and not as that of the Lord in us, we being simply co-operators; and we recognize the truths we obtain as light gained by our own studies, and not as light shed down from a Divine source through the higher firmament of the mind.

This is one of the stages of our progress which cannot possibly be avoided. We may hear the higher idea preached and fully assent to it, and yet we will fail to realize it. We will grow into that. But it is not an exceedingly vivified state. The waters of truth may flow into the mind but they are hardly *living* waters. Light may shed its radiance upon the firmament of the spiritual mind, but it is scarcely *living* light. The soul may be touched with the higher truth, and its affections may be stirred to reach forth for the higher life, but it cannot, in a proper sense, be called, as yet, a *living* soul.

Now in this parable of regeneration, the lower state I have thus delineated is described by the vegetation created on the third day; but the higher state, when one is conscious of all his truth as the light of God and of all his goodness as the influence of the Lord, is described and represented by the living soul which the waters brought forth.

For our present purpose, I prefer the exactly literal translation of the original Hebrew given by Swedenborg to that of the authorized version. In the latter it reads, "Let the waters bring forth abundantly the moving creature that hath life." But the accurate rendering is, to give in English the precise force of the Hebrew words, "Let the waters bring forth abundantly the creeping thing, the living soul." It is this term, "living soul," which gives force and point to the idea. The regenerating individual becomes now, in this stage of progress, a truly living soul. In a certain sense, vegetation, indeed, has life, but it is an utterly unconscious life. It represents, in a happy manner, one's first efforts at good action, because he is unconscious of the Lord's presence in those first efforts. They are not truly and spiritually alive, because the conscious feeling is that their motive springs originate in himself. The Lord's higher influence is not at all perceptible in them.

But when the man essays to speak and think from a genuine faith, and to will and act from real love, he then begins to be, in an elevated spiritua sense, a *living soul*. His first beginnings of religous life were mere spiritual vegetation, a state in which he possesses no consciousness of the Lord as the life of all that is true and good within him, just as natural vegetation has no consciousness whatever of the life that makes it lovely. But in the advanced stage to which I now refer all this is changed. He feels a consciousness that all his life—that all his truth and goodness, is but the Lord's influence within him, just as the things of animate creation—the beasts and birds—move on in the conscious enjoyment of the physical life they possess.

This is not a difficult thought to grasp even though one may not have arrived at so high a state. We well know how common it is to move along through life just as though there were no living soul of God within it. We buy, we sell, we sing, we dance, we hold social converse, we perform religious acts, just as though *we* did it all. Yet the very blood is coursing through our veins, the heart is beating in rythmic cadence, breath comes and goes with each expansion and contraction of the lungs, without a conscious effort of our own; for there is a life within and behind it all which works away, with no consultation on the subject with our thought and will. In mental life it is the same. The mind works on and man has not the power to stop it. He may lead it, guide it, but even a self-inflicted bullet through the brain will not cause the throbbings of a once created mind to cease. It still works on and it works forever. It is the energy of God within and behind this individuality of ours. Yet who thinks of it? Who takes conscious cognizance of its presence? Who does otherwise than live and work, as though this life was all his own? True we have individuality, and we influence the course, each one of his own life, but who looks behind, in common thought, at the concealed springs of existence which lie within that individuality?

So we look forth upon the beauties of the floral world, or upward at the sunlit sky. The grass is growing beneath our feet, the brilliant flowers of a thousand hues adorn our garden beds, the luscious fruit is hanging from the bended boughs, the sky is filled with light for our coming and going steps, and displays all forms of beauty to our eyes. But is there any conscious thought as we see, and walk, and work amid them all, that the Lord's never ceasing inflow of Divine life is pushing up the grass on which we tread, is painting the blossoms with the pure white or flaming red, with gold or azure blue, is pouring the juicy current into the hanging fruit, or is making the world radiant with the light which illumines our daily walk?

Do we walk forth with the consciousness that it is God who by his ceaseless influence lights up the sun, and warms the soil, and forms the rain, and as the great supernal Law lives in all law, and universally throbs through all the laws which make and keep this universe, from its greatest to its least things, so wonderfully grand and so transcendently beautiful?

Nay, we scarcely ever think of it. Yet if any wise mentor calls our attention to the fact, if we read in some reverent book or in the Word of God that we are indebted to the Lord of the universe for all that glory of natural creation which every where surrounds us, for our knowledge, our understanding, our love, for the truth we gain and the good we get, then, perhaps, we will acknowledge that it is so. But the idea is not an ever present, conscious, *living* idea, which lifts us in our daily life above ourselves, and which feels the breath of the Lord's mercy and love in every act of a busy life, and along every path of a righteous walk.

But when you have arrived at that stage of spiritual life which is represented in the parable by the creation of the *living soul*, then the situation changes. Then you begin to bear about with you the consciousness of the Divine origin of all you have and enjoy, and of the Divine presence in all you are. I do not mean that your active thoughts will at all times be actively centered on God, or that in all your discourse you will be ever repeating your belief in his agency, operation or influence. Spiritual life is an eminently practical thing. It does not ask you to be ever dreaming to the neglect of your work, or ever ecstatic to the point of forgetting that you live *in* the world *for* the world. But I do mean that you will feel the Lord as you linger amid his blessings just as you know the presence of the sunlight as you walk the ways of earth, just as you realize the moon and stars as above you when by their radiance you travel the paths of night, just as you revel in the perfume of the flowers or the new mown hay, when you pass through gardens or meadows. You may be conversing on utterly incongruous themes; your thoughts may run deeply on the cares and questions your worldly duties lay before you; you may be at play or at work; yet they are an ever present, ever conscious influence, which is as realistic as the sunshine which surrounds you and as certain as that you live.

So may your spiritual life be saturated with the consciousness of the Lord's presence and ownership and influence in all the good you will or do, in all the truth you think or say, in all your faithfulness in work, steadfastness in duty, sincerity in office, purity in principle, glowing love of use; yea in every ripple of laughter, in every enjoyment or pleasure, in every innocent pastime. And though thought does not outwardly nor actively think it, nor speech actually frame it into words, the heart is full of it, and thought and speech will glow with it at the instant some little circumstance seems to call them forth. You live amid the sphere of its radiance and you bask in the sunlight of its everlasting presence.

This state, however, is one of great spiritual elevation. The fifth stage of regeneration, the fifth day of the new creation of the soul, only marks its beginnings. The state is one which only the highest angels of heaven enjoy in its full perfection. Happy we, if we can gain such brightening glimpses of its truth, such occasional broad experiences of its reality, as will lead us to yearn for its presence more and more. To love a thing is to get it in the end. For love will compass all things; it will tear down impediments; it will break through barriers; it will restlessly work until it gains the object loved. Love for mental states once experienced, for heart-conditions which meet the Lord's approval, wil gain, in the end, their permanent possession.

So in this fifth stage of progress toward a perfect life, we gain our conscious beginnings of the happiness which the soul may possess in obtaining a genuine faith in the Lord, and in realizing a love for Him and his words of life. In the fourth stage, the sun, moon and stars—love, faith and knowledge, first lit our shining way. In the fifth stage, the soul begins, for the first time, in a really spiritual sense, to live. Our love, faith and knowledge now begin to become really living energies. They give spiritual vitality to all we desire, think and do. True, they will not prove to be of the most intensely vital kind even yet. Still there will be stumbling and falling. Old states which are of earth, earthy, will, at times, cloud, for a brief while, the life. Thoughts of the flesh pots of Egypt will, occasionally, lure us back to our worldly ways. But, notwithstanding this, we will have here experienced a consciousness of the Lord's presence and life in all things about us, in all we have and are, in our faculties and powers, in our knowledges and affections, in our aspirations and desires, which will create a longing for the time when we can rest forever in Him. To rest in Him is to rest in this consciousness of his perpetual influence and presence.

To be alive then, spiritually, is to feel the Lord's presence and influence as energizing our onward way. To vegetate, spiritually, is to acknowledge the fact after an intelligent manner, but to lack the conscious feeling of that presence—the realized sphere of that influence. In this we now see more clearly by comparison the two symbolisms—the springing forth of vegetation on the third day and the bringing forth of *living* creatures on the fifth day. The one is the correspondence under which the earthly phases of regenerative life are described, the other, the spiritual figure under which this later and higher phase of progress is set forth. The one typifies that which in its degree and order is beautiful but inanimate, the other that which is on an altogether higher plane, and animate or truly living.

It is said in the parable, "Let *the waters bring forth* the creeping thing, the living soul." We have had occasion to note in previous lectures, that waters, throughout the Scriptures, are symbols of truths. In repeating this it must, of course, be remembered that the truths so symbolized are of a spiritual character only. Those which the Lord gives, those which teach of Himself and his ways, those which tell of the immortality of the soul and the nature of the future life, those which teach us of regeneration and the true path of Christian progress—those only constitute the water of life described in the Revelation as proceeding out of the throne of God and the Lamb—those only are the waters which can come in unto the soul.

It is truth—the truth Divine, which brings forth every good for man. Looking at the matter from a natural point of view merely, we can do no work, we can be useful in no employment, we can minister to our fellows in no profession, until we learn the natural truths which cover that profession or work. Much more is this spiritually so. Our minds are elevated to the Lord by every truth we gain with regard to Him. Our characters grow stronger in the study of his nature and character. We become regenerate, and thus fulfil the destiny for which we were born, by learning the truths He gives us in his Word and by living in their light. We become spiritual minded by coming into their spirit. "Let the waters bring forth" means, therefore, in the language of spiritual symbolism, "Let the truths you have gained bring forth their appropriate results." You have learned much, it is now time you live much. You have arrived at a stage of regeneration where the truths you have acquired must become *living* truths.

This shows the importance of penetrating to their utmost depths, so far as in us lies, the Divine truths we gain. While it is a fact that truth, without a correlative leading on to life, is worthless and dead, it is also a fact that the more truths with regard to the Lord and eternal life we can acquire, the more we will be enabled to live spiritually, regeneratively, usefully.

So it is said, "Let the waters bring forth *abundantly*." The broader the waters the greater the abundance of life they can bring forth and support. The broader our field of spiritual truth, the broader the field of useful, and therefore spiritual, works we will find spreading forth to view. Indeed, the very attempt to live what we know, makes the life more abounding in results of good, and this without limit and without stint.

But it is said, "Let the waters bring forth abundantly *the creeping thing, the living soul.*" Yes; it is to the intent that we may become *living souls* that all this work goes on. Of what avail our knowledge, our activity, our energy, our enthusiasm, unless it goes forth at last into genuine spiritual life? Of what avail the possession of a soul unless that soul is made alive in the light of God? It is something to be born; but it is something more to be born again. It is something to have this body live, but it is infinitely more to have the soul alive. Life is God; and God is life. That life may be filtered through all the lower strata of thought and purpose, so that it partake of all the filthiness which inheres in stagnant things; or it may be obtained at the fountain head, pure as the spring from whence it flows, sparkling as the light that flashes from its spray. The nearer we get to the source, the purer the life. The purer the life we draw, the more eternally living the soul. When the waters of God within the man bring forth the *living soul*—the soul as a thing to all intents, in its Divine purity, alive—man then begins to be a man.

The living soul, however, is here called a *creeping thing*, because the man at this stage of regeneration, can scarcely be said to walk erect, but only to creep. "You must learn to creep before you can walk" is an old adage. It is as true of regeneration as of physical life. Though we have learned now, in a higher sense, to live, though we have gained a consciousness of the Lord's life, though we begin to realize our goodness and truth not as our own but as the Lord's in us, this life, this consciousness, this realization, in comparison with what they will be, are still feeble. Before, we were not even living souls. Though now endued with life, we are yet mere babes in Christ. We can creep, not walk. This is at first; afterward we will do better.

It is worthy of notice how gradually this parable of regeneration leads us on. It recognizes no sudden changes in our gathering strength. Like the growth of a tree, however certain it may be, it is imperceptible. We cannot look into ourselves and say, "So we were yesterday and so much further we are to-day." Much less can we say, "We were a child of the devil a moment ago, but at this minute we are a child of God." But it is development, unfolding imperceptibly, but not ceasing. It is creeping before walking, learning before living, the one merging by invisible openings into the other, and that all the way through.

And now it follows on in our text concerning the birds. "Let the waters bring forth abundantly the creeping thing, the living soul, and let the fowl fly above the earth upon the faces of the expanse of the heavens." I use here again the more literal rendering from the Hebrew which Swedenborg gives. The authorized version reads as though the waters brought forth the fowl; but in the Hebrew of the original it is not so.

Birds in the symbolism of Scripture signify our thought. They do so because the thought can soar up and away from its surroundings, even piercing the realms of spirit, of heaven, and of God, as birds fly above the earth and waters into the firmament above. "Let fowl fly above the earth" means, Let the thoughts of the regenerating man now rise above earthly things, above those that occupy the lower mind. "Upon the faces of the expanse of the heavens," or "in the open firmament of heaven" means, Let them rise to heavenly and eternal themes, and soar amid the regions of the spiritual mind with broad and far-reaching views of the higher truth of God, as the bird in its upward flight broadens its scope of vision the higher it goes.

And then it is said, "God created great whales (properly leviathans) and every living soul that creepeth which the waters brought forth abundantly after its kind, and every winged fowl after its kind." The Leviathan, as the largest inhabitant of the deep, symbolizes knowledge in its general or largest principles. The more alive we become to the spiritual side of things, the more we gather what we know into general principles, and get the particulars into order and arrangement in the thought. Spiritual knowledge becomes thus no irrational faith, no unformed scheme, no vapid array of meaningless phrases, but a grand scheme of spiritual philosophy, complete in all its parts, beautiful in its symmetry, spiritually approved by the reason of man, and worthy of God. The leviathans of the mind, its grand conclusions, its large and fully rounded philosophy, always come last. The more alive our truths are the grander they become in character and scope. Not until we enter into *living* relations with God, do the truth-waters of the soul bring forth their leviathans of thought.

Such is the New-Church interpretation of what is related in the parable concerning the fifth day of Creation. As we ascend the mountains of regeneration the view becomes more broad and beautiful. If life is so good on the merely natural plane, on the spiritual how infinitely more lovely! To come into states of elevation where all we know becomes instinct with the life of God, and every truth, with gentle light, points out some duty to our fellow man; where the whole realm of mind is alive with spiritual affections, resolves and principles; where the soul is innately conscious of the Lord and his influences as urging them into every form of loving energy of good; where the thoughts soar upward into realms and spheres unknown to man the animal, and gain broad vistas of diviner view, of which mere life for the world and self cannot in the most remote degree conceive—to come into such states of elevation throws, indeed, a new light upon the problem of life and man. Then we know what life is worth. Then, truly, life is worth the living!

VI.

THE IMAGE OF GOD.

And God said, Let the earth bring forth the living creature after his kind, cattle, and creeping thing, and beast of the earth after his kind; and it was so. And God made the beast of the earth after his kind, and cattle after their kind, and every creeping thing that creepeth upon the earth after his kind: and God saw that it was good. And God said, Let us make man in our image after our likeness: and let them have dominion over the fish of the sea, and over the fowl of the air, and over the cattle, and over all the earth, and over every creeping thing that creepeth upon the earth. So God created man in his own image, in the image of God created he him; male and female created he them. And God blessed them, and God said unto them, Be fruitful and multiply, and replenish the earth and subdue it: and have dominion over the fish of the sea, and over the fowl of the air, and over every living thing that moveth upon the earth. And God said, Behold, I have given you every herb bearing seed, which is upon the face of all the earth, and every tree, in the which is the fruit of a tree yielding seed; to you it shall be for meat. And to every beast of the earth, and to every fowl of the air, and to every thing that creepeth upon the earth, wherein there is life, I have given every green herb for meat: and it was so. And God saw every thing that he had made, and, behold, it was very good. And the evening and the morning were the sixth day.—Gen. 1: 24-31.

IN five previous lectures, in review of the story of the creation, as contained in the first chapter of Genesis, we have traced the narrative in detail as a parable of the regeneration of the human mind. The five days were found to represent five advancing stages of spiritual progress, through which each individual must pass who seeks to gain the higher life. In other words, the states and experiences through which the regenerating man must pass are typified by the days of creation. He begins in a state of darkness with reference to spiritual things. The first advance which is made by his mind is into some light of truth, especially as to the higher value of a knowledge of God and eternal life. The second is to gain some ability to comprehend spiritual ideas. The third is to commence a reformation of the outward life under their influence. The fourth is to acquire that faith in the Lord, and that love for Him which is necessary to a truly spiritual walk with God. The fifth is to lead a true and noble life under a strong rational consciousness— an inward absolute intellectual conviction, of the glory and beauty of this higher faith and love.

These steps are each, in their turn, pronounced by the Lord to be good. And they are. But what is good in its degree is not always the perfection of its kind. A seed hid away in the damp, dark earth is good. The first shoot it sends upward into the realm of light is good. The noble trunk, its pillar of strength, is good. The spreading branches reaching far and wide around are good. So is its leafage.

So is its flowering. But its great perfection and its final use are developed only when it has come to that stage of growth wherein it is able to bring forth fruit. The fruit is the end for which the tree was designed by its Creator. Each step of its development is good as a stage of progress; but it has fulfilled its destiny, it has reached for the first time its highest perfection as a tree, when it becomes first fruit laden. This also, in its way, is a parable of man.

And so it was with the earth. Its incipient stages of creation were pronounced by the Lord to be good. When the dry land first made its appearance above the waters, it was good. When the land brought forth vegetation, although animate life was still unknown, it was good. Good when the mists cleared away, and sun, moon and stars shone down for its greater and more glorious light; good when the fish began to people its waters, the birds to fly in its atmospheres, and the beasts to roam its grassy plains. But it was not called *very* good until it had advanced to a condition when it was fit for the habitation of man, and so fulfilled the object of its creation.

The earth, in the narrative, is used as a symbol of the mind of man. The regeneration of the mind goes on by steps parallel with the development of the tree, or the creation of the earth. Here again each degree of progress is good and our Lord so pronounces it. But it is good only as one step more toward perfection, and not in the sense of perfection itself. Our first religious light is good. So are our first clear conceptions of faith in God and love to Him; so are our first creeping steps under a clear intellectual life of faith and love. But the consummation and crown of it all is such an affection for good and for God, as springs from the Lord as the enthroned life, soul and centre of the being. Our desires, thoughts and acts are then saturated with the Spirit of God. We are not engulfed in the great ocean of Divinity, nor do we lose our individuality in being merged into the overwhelming glory of God, according to the Buddhist doctrine of Nirvana. On the contrary, the higher we rise in our spiritual manhood, the more distinctly individual we become. While, therefore, in coming into this much to be desired state, our personality is more and more keenly felt, our trust in, and reliance on, the Lord, and our perception of Him as our light, our life, our all, become also more and more inwardly realized.

Nor is this the ordinary doctrine of sanctification nor anything like it. The accepted theory of what is commonly called sanctification is, that the individual becomes holy. The Scripture, when interpreted in its true spirit, does not recognize that any man can ever become holy. God alone is holy. We may walk in his light, we may accept the influences of his Spirit, we may act as his stewards in dispensing to others the bounties which are by Him so plentifully prepared; but the light is his, the Spirit is his, the bounties are of his supplying. Therefore, true regeneration makes us sweet and gentle clothes us with genuine humility, strips us of all pride of holiness, expels every vestige of assumed sanctity. It draws no long faces; it makes no large pretences. Genuine regeneration never dwells, even secretly or in the lightest thought, on its own merit, on how good it has become, or compares itself in respect to righteousness in any way with its fellow man. It knows that "there is none good but one, God."

The doctrine of sanctification, as it is usually held, dwells much upon one's feelings, upon his states of ecstasy, upon his exuberant exaltations above the things of the world. Its essential theory is not so much outward use as inward transport. True regeneration throws its energies into uses and lets feelings take care of themselves. Or, more properly, its thoughts are directed to doing, and doing under the right spirit, and it leaves all other things with God. Happiness comes it is true. But it is not the selfish happiness of a contemplation of one's own blessedness, but that which exists in making others happy. It is not a feeling of inward bliss indulged for the sake of the bliss, but it is the satisfaction of seeing the good work go on, the heavenly cause succeed, in the sphere of one's own activities and in all the world around.

So far as we can understand the mind of God, his infinite blessedness must arise from his infinite activities. No pent of fires of self-satisfied glory burn within his soul. All He is goes forth. He creates worlds; his ceaseless going forth of life sustains them. Creation never stops. In a single world once made, it is seed-time and harvest forever, an endless succession of efforts on the part of the Divine energies for the benefit of man. He creates man; and again it is a ceaseless working on the spiritual plane of his being for his constant elevation. He not only forms the world of nature and man as a physical being, but He forms the world of souls and man as a spiritual being. The heavens are studded with stars. Each star is a sun like that which rules our own small planetary system. Around each revolves a circle of planets peopled with human beings, or some, perhaps, preparing for that end. The more powerful they make our telescopes the more of these planetary systems come forth to view. No man and no number of men, improve your telescopes as you may, will ever count the myriads of worlds in this grand universe, which are made to rear a human progeny for heaven. And as age succeeds age a ceaseless procession of human souls is passing from every earth of this immeasurable universe of planetary spheres into the infinite world beyond. The grandeur of the thought is overwhelming. And in every time of illimitable space and in every state of each one's life in all these worlds, into the universe of nature and into that of spirit, these Divine activities are flowing, creating, sustaining, developing, recreating.

God is, therefore, not a self-glorifying Being. His happiness is in his goings forth for others, not in the contemplation of his own greatness. If we, then, are actuated by his Spirit, our happiness is never in self-satisfaction. Sanctification in any such sense is a delusion and a snare. The more we forget ourselves in our energies of use in the field of our surroundings, the more we work in the spirit of the Lord. The essence of the religion of the Scriptures, under New-Church interpretation, is altruism not egoism. And of all forms of egoism that which claims the highest seat in the synagogue of the Lord is the shabbiest and the worst, and the very one which was most condemned of Christ.

We are, in our reflections upon this parable of regeneration, approaching its highest point. It is well that we should not misunderstand its character, nor mingle it with the crude misconceptions of the day. I repeat, thus, that in the highest stage of regeneration, the Lord becomes the enthroned life, soul, and centre of the being. Our desires, thoughts and acts, are then saturated with his Spirit and his presence. But this spirit is wonderfully altruistic, not egoistic. It wanders forth to others and forgets self, except as our well being and advance is necessary to the great good in view. This state of mind is the end for which we were born. And we have not attained the symmetry of true manhood, do not bring forth fruits of a fully regenerate life, are not, in the strict sense, *men* until it has come to this pass with us. But before proceeding further on this line of thought, let us consider, in the order in which they occur, the words of the parable concerning the sixth day.

"*And God said, Let the earth bring forth the living creature after his kind, cattle and creeping thing, and beast of the earth after his kind, and it was so. And God made the beast of the earth after his kind, and cattle after their kind, and every creeping thing that creepeth upon the earth after his kind: and God saw that it was good.*

As we had occasion to see in our last lecture, the *fifth* day of creation represented that stage of regeneration where, under the influence of a deep faith in the Lord and an earnest love for Him, the beginnings of a truly spiritual life are made. The earth was said to bring forth the *living soul* as a symbol of the mind making, in a spiritual sense, its first living efforts. In other words, the soul became, in a strict sense, truly *living* for the first time. The living soul was called a creeping thing, because our first living efforts at a spiritual life, are, as all first efforts are, infant like, creeping rather than walking. The *birds* were representative of our *thoughts* and conceptions of spiritual things, now of a living character and of a kind, which, bird-like, soar into the loftier regions of the mind and gain grand views of life and its real purposes.

Now, however, beasts are created. Beasts are symbols of affections. The creation of the beasts on the earth represents the creation of truly spiritual affections in the mind. In the fifth state of regeneration we have living conceptions of the Lord and his truths, and from those living ideas we think and discourse after a spiritual manner. We have deep faith in the Lord and a clear insight into the question of what love to the Lord means. We live spiritually, but we love because we have faith. Our faith is the primary element of our life and our love is secondary. We are more on the intellectual plane of religion yet, although our intellectuality is a living one, than we are on the love plane. But in the sixth state all this is changed. Where belief was before the predominant principle, now affection rules. We no longer love because we believe, but we believe because we love.

This is illustrated by many not uncommon experiences. In the beginning of a genuine friendship, for instance, we have learned to have so thorough a belief in a person that we cannot help loving him. We have studied his character and principles; we have trusted often and have never been deceived, and our faith ripens into a love based upon it. But afterward, when we know our friend still better, and have touched the deeper chords of his nature, and have found our sympathies intertwined on the most vital points, love becomes the controlling element of our friendship. We do not now so much love him because we have thorough faith in him, but we have faith in him because our sympathies touch at every vital point, thus because we love him.

To believe in the Lord and the life which He commands, because we have gained a clear and living knowledge of Him and it, and to love them from such faith, is a near approach to the goal of regeneration. But to enter into such an intimate communion with Him that we are all aglow with a loving realization of his nature, and thence to have a most perfect faith in Him, *is* regeneration. The one is the flowering of the beautiful tree of life; the other is its fruitage. The first is represented in the parable under consideration by the creation of creeping things and birds; the second by the creation of beasts.

That beasts are symbols of the human affections is not only a fact easily deduced from Scripture, but it is a remnant of the ancient method of speaking which remains to this day. This is true both in an evil sense and a good sense. The bears and the wolves and the foxes of the world are the rude, the cruel, and the cunning. The swine of the world are those whose affections are set on sensual things. But the lion is the type of courage, the ox of meekness, the sheep of innocence. So the pure and gentle followers of the Lord are called in the Scripture the sheep of his pasture. He who is thirsting for the higher truth, not yet attained, is likened to the hart panting after the water brooks. And every animal is used by name in reference to its peculiar spiritual symbolism. So when the Psalm says, "Praise ye the Lord, ye beasts and all cattle," it is not that the dumb brutes are literally called upon to offer praises to their Creator, but that the affections of the heart, of which the beasts and the cattle are the symbols, are to go up in praise to Him. Thus also here, in the words of the Creation-parable, by the creation of the beasts of the earth is symbolized the bringing forth the most exalted spiritual affections of the mind.

But the culmination of all this is in the creation of man. To this end, from the beginning, every thing has pointed. For this purpose every thing else has been made. As this is true of the progress of earth, so it is true of the advance of the human mind. Every preparatory stage of regeneration has been for the sake of the one beyond. Each and all have been for the sake of the final outcome. Whatever has taken place, little as at the time it has seemed so to the person, has been a step to lead still further upward toward the summit life. All that has happened through a long and eventful life, each trivial incident, each, even the most obscure, of its surroundings, each changing state, was nothing in and of itself. It was valuable only in its bearings on that which was to come. All knowledge, all study, all discipline, was worthless, except so far as it led, directly or indirectly, to that. The Lord's call to each and every human being that was ever born is, Be a MAN.

Now we know very well what this, in ordinary parlance, means. Be courageous! be earnest! be faithful! be honest! But in the Lord's view a MAN is much more than this. It is the Lord alone, who, in the highest signification of the term, may properly be called MAN. He only, in the most eminent perfection, embodies all that is human. He is perfect Wisdom, perfect Love, perfect Truth, perfect Goodness. He alone possesses, in consummate and limitless measure, will and understanding, affection and intellect. He is THE MAN. We become men only so far as we are created, or reborn, into his image and likeness.

And here it will be well to remark, that in the older tongues—the Hebrew, Greek and Latin, there is a peculiarity unknown to those of modern times. They possess, each of them, two words, of different form, which we are obliged to translate by the one word *man*. The Hebrew term *ish* means man as distinguished from woman—a masculine being. But the Hebrew term *Adam* means man in the broad sense including male and female, just as we would say, "Man is mortal," meaning that every human being, without distinction of sex, is mortal. Where the term man, is used in the first chapter of Genesis, it is *Adam*—man in the abstract—man as of either sex. This relieves the text of the idea, sometimes foolishly advanced, that the Bible is man's book, not woman's, because it speaks so much of man. The trouble lies in the poverty of the English language in reference to that one expression. We possess no separate word by which to translate *Adam*. Man, therefore, thus used, includes both sexes.

The declaration of God, then, "Let us make man in our image, after our likeness," does not refer to one male being, but to mankind at large. Nor does it mean, in its spiritual, symbolic sense, the first formation on earth of the human race. It has reference to the rebirth of man into the image and likeness of God. It is not said, simply, "Let us make man," but it is said, "Let us make man in our image, after our likeness." Nor, repeating the phrase, does it simply say, "So God created man," but it says, "So God created man in his own image." The entire reference is, in its parable meaning, not to God's creating a physical man, but to his forming him into a likeness of Himself.

We have seen that, strictly speaking, God is the only man. We become men, not by rising to his level—we cannot do that—but by receiving his light and love so perfectly and fully, that the self-life is removed from our consciousness and its activities. By the self-life, however, as a term thus used, is to be understood, not our individuality, nor the distinctive recognition of our free agency as rational beings, nor the necessity of self protection, support and effort, but life for the sake of self.

Before we are regenerated, we are not men; we are only in the semblance and shape of men. We are not in the human form, but full of animal propensities, which, if extraneous pressure were removed, would level us to an equality with the brutes. We become men only as we advance into the likeness of God; in other words, only as we become inwardly like Him. So long as we are still only working up to the highest standard, although we have reached the sixth stage of regeneration, and although we may properly be called spiritual men, we are only images of Him. When we reach the highest state and come fully under his influences—are filled indeed with his life and love, then we become likenesses of Him. So while, indeed, it is here said, "Let us create man in our image after our likeness," it is added, referring to the work of the sixth state, "So God created man in his own image, in the image of God created he him." Man does not really become a likeness of God until his seventh and highest stage of regeneration.

But it is added, "Male and female created he them." The literal meaning of this I pass without comment. But in its spiritual meaning, it is to be observed that every man, and woman too, is, in regeneration, created male and female. That is to say, in the mind of each person there exists the masculine and feminine element. The masculine element of the mind is intellect or understanding; the feminine is affection or will. In the male, there is, or ought to be, no lack of affection, but reason or intellect should be the ruling principle. In the woman there is, or ought to be, no lack of intellect, but love or affection should be the ruling principle. It is not always so, perhaps, but so it will be where the person of either sex is in just order of mind.

So each one of all mankind is, in a certain sense, male *and* female. Each has intellect *and* affection. And in each both of these sides of the nature are to be regenerated. When, therefore, it is said, "In the image of God created he him, male and female created he them," the words are to be understood in this symbolic or spiritual sense. In this sixth stage of regeneration we have been, what we had not been before, created into the image of God. But this creation is not a partial one; it is of the masculine and the feminine elements of our nature alike. That is to say, our *reason* and *understanding* are advanced to that stage wherein we perceive all things of life spiritually, or see its spiritual meaning in its every phase; and our *affections* are advanced to that stage where they are placed upon the Lord and spiritual things. True, life in the world compels them to go forth to natural things; but now they do it in a spiritual manner only, and for the sake of spiritual ends. Thus the masculine element of the nature, the intellect, views all things in the Lord's light, and the feminine element, the affection, loves all things from spiritual and eternal considerations.

It is said, "Be fruitful and multiply, and replenish the earth and subdue it." Construing this spiritually, it is to be understood thus: that when at last the mind comes into the image of genuine manhood, its understandings of spiritual truth will indefinitely multiply, and its love of good will become wonderfully fruitful in spiritual works. In the beginnings of regeneration the mind's understandings of the truths concerning God, heaven, and eternal life, are feeble indeed and few. In its outcomes they multiply and grow strong beyond any thing that lower states can conceive of. In the beginnings of regeneration, the spiritual love is but feebly fruitful. In its outcomes, its fruit of good works and of ability to accomplish them has developed beyond all calculation. It is not the man, as a physical being, who is commanded to be fruitful and multiply, but it is the spiritual manhood of the mind. It is also commanded to "replenish the earth." To replenish is to fill again. The earth still typifies the mind. In the course of regeneration, the latter has cast out its false opinions and ignoble loves. It is to be replenished with spiritual ideas and heavenly loves. The command also goes forth to man to "subdue" the earth. This means that the new manhood is to subdue all its lower principles and desires, and to bring all portions of the mind into due subjection to its high behests.

And now man is commanded to have dominion over the fish of the sea, and over the fowl of the air, and over the cattle, and over all the earth, and over every creeping thing that creepeth upon the earth. The regenerated understanding and will, the intellect and affection, which have now become an image of God, are, at this stage of regeneration, to assume the dominion. It was the lower nature which previously ruled. It was self and the world—vanity, ambition, greed of power, lust of gain, desire of approbation, sensuous pleasure, or whatever the main spring of action might have been, which had hitherto borne rule. But now it is MAN—perfected manhood —manhood regenerated both as to intellect and affection, regenerated in both its masculine and feminine phases, which is to rule the whole realm of the mind.

The true man is the regenerated nature. This is to have dominion over whatever in the mind is symbolized by the fish of the sea, the fowl of the air, the cattle, all the earth, and every thing that creepeth upon the earth. The fish of the sea are the knowledges in the memory, the fowl of the air the thoughts which float through the atmosphere of the mind, the cattle the affections of the heart, all the earth the entire realm of mind, and every creeping thing that creepeth upon the earth, the instincts and ideas that lay close to the earth in the very natural duties and pleasures which a life in the world compel us to perform and enjoy. These are the things over which the man, the regenerated manhood, are to have and hold dominion. Once these things, in their unregenerate phases, ruled him. Now, he is to rule them.

To carry the idea a step higher; in the fully regenerated state, the whole nature is under the dominion of the Lord, who is, *par excellence*, THE MAN! It may also be said that the whole mind, with whatever is within it, is under the dominion of the regenerate nature, in which the Lord resides and of which He has gained control. The individual, however, is still left in perfect freedom, notwithstanding this control of the Lord. But it is a freedom in which the soul has, voluntarily and forever, chosen the Lord as his law, his love, his guide to all things good.

The concluding words of the chapter refer to the food which the Lord has provided for man and beast. The symbolism never halts or fails. The herb and the tree are symbols of the Lord's truth. This is the food of the spiritual nature. "Man shall not live by bread alone but by every word that proceedeth out of the mouth of God." Truth feeds the mind of the spiritual man. The herb yielding seed is the truth that yields abundant harvests of use and good. The tree in which is the fruit of a tree yielding seed is the same in a higher sense. But to every beast and fowl and creeping thing, every green herb was given for meat. All the affections and thoughts, and even the lower phases of duty which lie near our earthly work, are fed also by the Lord. The green herb is a lower form of food than the herb yielding seed. The term green conveys the idea of unripeness and lack of maturity. All phases of mind and life and duty have their food, their sustaining truths suited to their form and kind. The higher the phase the more spiritually mature the food, the lower the phase, the more spiritually crude.

Well, we have come to the end of the description of the sixth state of regeneration, as set forth in the parable of creation. The regenerating individual has developed into a true spiritual manhood. The Lord has done the work all the way through; the man has only co-operated. Therefore the expression "And God made" is always used. The idea is not difficult to gain. It is like the case of a diligent gardener. He knows that it is the sun and rain which really causes his plants to come to perfection. Yet he digs, and weeds, and prunes, and trains, and waters. Without his co-operation the garden would have remained in a sorry state indeed. He recognizes that his co-operative work is necessary; but he does not pretend to claim that he has made the plants grow, when he knows so well, that the sun and rain and dew performed the work.

Thus it is with man. As a cultivator of the garden of his own mind, he must weed out his propensities to evil, loosen the soil of his naturally hard spirit, prune his bad habits, train into upward growth his vines of desire and thought, and water every heart plant with the truths of God's own Word. Yet he knows, and the more he progresses the more certainly he feels, and in the end he fully realizes, that it was the Lord by his shedding forth of light and love upon the mind, that it was the Lord by the softening influences of the rains and dews of his gentle Spirit, who really wrought the wondrous change. Yes; it it is the Lord above who has really lifted the man up, from the voidness and darkness of his merely natural state, into this condition of living, loving, God-like manhood, which is the very image of Himself.

This elevated state may be far above the place whereon we stand. Our conceptions of it may be dreamy and dim. To our consciousness, it may seem more like a fairy land of imagination than a state we can veritably realize and enjoy. The mists of a worldly life may hide or render hazy and obscured its mountain tops. Yet it is well to look up. It is well to have even indistinct visions of lovely things. He who aims low hits no higher than the level of his mark. Even a dim dream of more elevated things is better than to rest in the sensuous valleys of worldly life, unconscious of a higher hope. A dream of wakeful hours is a thought idealized. It is at least a quickening sign. And that dream, by dwelling on it, may become a recognized want. And a want once felt may develop into a fixed purpose. And every fixed purpose ends, in spiritual things, at least, in the possession of that which we fain would have.

The Lord by quiet methods guides us through all the mazy ways of life. He only asks a fixed purpose and a faithful walk in the paths that He sets before us. No matter how rough or uncongenial they may be, work on, toil on, do the nearest good at hand and do it well. Believing, trusting, loving, and yet, it may be, ignorant, amid the bustle of this weary world, of just where we spiritually stand;—dying, we may find that we have reached the summits of celestial manhood in the better world to come.

VII.

THE REST OF GOD.

Thus the heavens and the earth were finished, and all the host of them. And on the seventh day God ended his work which he had made; and he rested on the seventh day from all his work which he had made. And God blessed the seventh day and sanctified it; because that in it he had rested from all his work which God created and made.—Gen. ii: 1-3.

The subject of the Sabbath or seventh day has received a large amount of discussion and attention. It has usually, however, been rather from a natural than a spiritual point of view. Those who imagine that external observances contain, in themselves, a large amount of religion, and that salvation depends in a great measure on our faithful adherence to outward forms as such, would naturally be much exercised over questions of this nature. If their future destiny really depends on whether they are sprinkled or immersed in baptism, on whether the ecclesiastic who administers it is in direct line of authority from the apostles or no, or on whether their worship to God is offered up on Saturday or Sunday, certainly it is most important to determine, in these matters, which is right and which is wrong.

But there are those who believe, with all their

hearts, in that most significant declaration of Christ, "God is a spirit, and they who worship him must worship him in spirit and in truth." It is the spirit and the truth with which one worships, not the day or the form, which is of real significance. Forms, of course, have their value or they would not be given. But that value can only be estimated by a full understanding of the spiritual purpose for which they were ordained. In ignorance of this we necessarily mistake the outward form for the inward reality, and we necessarily lay great stress on the correctness of the minor details of the form, to the great neglect of that spirit and purpose for which alone it was given. Let us apply this idea to the question of the Sabbath.

The Sabbath was instituted—so it is stated in Exodus—in commemoration of the fact that "in six days the Lord made heaven and earth, the sea, and all that in them is, and rested the seventh day. Wherefore," it is added, "The Lord blessed the Sabbath day and hallowed it."

Now science has proved as conclusively as it is possible for science to prove anything, that the world, so far from having been made in six days, was many hundred thousand years in formation. And another truth has become equally well established, to wit, that many of the stars of heaven were created at a period inconceivably more ancient than that of the creation of the earth. Why, there are stars whose light has taken millions of years to reach this planet. They must, therefore, have been created millions of years before the earth.

Thus when the Scripture says that "the heavens and the earth were finished, and all the host of them," as the result of six days work on the part of God; when, indeed, it allows six days for the creation of the earth, but only one for the myriad stars of heaven, it presents a problem which the undeniable deductions of science positively contradict. It is, certainly, an unpleasant predicament for the intelligent mind which fervently loves the Word of God, and yet cannot close its eyes to proven facts.

There is a way in which an attempt has been made to avoid the difficulty. It is said that the Hebrew word which is here translated *day* may mean not only a period of twenty-four hours, but also an indefinite cycle of time; and that therefore we have a perfect right to accept that usage of the term which will vindicate the consistency and justify the scientific accuracy of the Bible. That the original Hebrew term may under certain circumstances bear such a construction is, perhaps, true. But we are confronted with the fact that the Lord, in giving the ten commandments, expressly says that we are to keep each seventh day holy because that in six days He made the heavens and the earth and all that in them is, and rested on the seventh day. So if the Hebrew word for day in its relation to creation means an indefinite period of many thousands of years, it forces us to the inference that we are to keep every period of thousands of years each as our Sabbath. This is a conclusion so palpably contrary to the Lord's meaning that the very statement of it contains its own refutation.

Far be it from us to endeavor to cast ridicule or discredit on the holy Word of God. On the contrary my only desire is to elevate it from the absurd position in which it is placed by a baldly literal interpretation, to one which consistency can endorse and rationality can grasp. It is unquestionably true that the development of the earth into a world fit for the habitation of man was about in the order indicated in the first chapter of Genesis. And it is a note-worthy fact that it should be so, considering that when this book was written the science of geology was unknown. But it is still more true that this chapter was never designed as an account of the literal creation of the heavens, the earth, or the heavenly hosts. It is an allegory or parable. It is written in the Divine style which is always symbolic. It was composed, by inspiration, at a time when men were nearer the original sources of language as it came to them freshly from God, and when, therefore, the Divine language was better understood than now. It is enough for us to be satisfied that the expressions are correctly used *as symbols*. So far as they agree with science, well. So far as they do not, it is of no consequence in respect to the Lord's purpose in giving the narrative, provided only the symbolism is divinely correct, and the spiritual lesson conveyed within it divinely true. This question of the true day of Sabbath we will find to be rationally solved, as we come to understand the spiritual meaning of the words in which allusion is made to the seventh day of creation. Indeed the whole Sabbath question rests upon these very words.

But first permit me for the last time to revert to the explanations which have been so thoroughly set forth in the six previous discourses of this series. We have learned that the narrative is an allegory of the regeneration of the human mind. The heaven and the earth were found to be symbols of the two minds of man, or if you prefer the expression, the two regions of his mind, its heavenly and its earthly, or in other words, its spiritual and its natural. Creation symbolizes the regeneration, that is the rebirth, or new creation of the spiritual nature. A day, in the spiritual sense, means a state. The six days of creation represent the six progressive states or stages of regeneration, from the mind's darkness and voidness as to spiritual things, in its original condition, to the state of perfect peace of mind and rest of heart which is the final result of its labors and struggles against all that is natural, earthly and low.

When our Lord says that the kingdom of God, or, as He elsewhere uses the expression, the kingdom of heaven, is within us, we can but conclude, that heaven, as a symbol, refers to the spiritual mind or nature of man. When we read in the Gospel of John, "He that is of the earth is earthly and speaketh earthly things," we cannot fail to observe that the earth is used as a type of the earthly or natural mind. When the Psalmist says, "Create in me a clean heart O God, and renew a right spirit within me," we know that he refers to the creation, that is, the regeneration, of the soul. When he declares, "A day in thy courts is better than a thousand," we are sure that he refers to a state of heart worship, and not to a literal twenty-four hours in the temple. Thus we know that these expressions, heaven, earth, creation, day, as well as all the others, *are* used in spiritual senses, in other portions of the Word of God. So when we come to this narrative of creation as an allegory of regeneration, we have but to apply them according to the manner in which they are plainly used to indicate spiritual ideas in other portions of Scripture, and the first chapter of Genesis is translated into its true spiritual meaning. Thus the Word of God is lifted from the mire of mere sensuous discussion, out of the region of literal confusion and inconsistency, into the clear, heavenly atmosphere of spiritual wisdom.

I return to these primary postulates again and again with reason. To those to whom truths of this nature are new, it must be "line upon line and precept upon precept." It is only by constant re-iteration that the idea becomes indelibly engraven on the mind. Let us now revert to our text.

Thus the heavens and the earth were finished and all the hosts of them. What does this mean in the light of all we have thus far learned? Simply that the spiritual mind and the natural mind, together with all the knowledges of spiritual things which appertain to them are now, at last, in the highest sense, regenerated. You will not forget that the heaven is the spiritual mind, the earth the natural mind, and the stars spiritual knowledges. Then as the creation signifies the regeneration, the finishing of creation refers to the completion of the work of regeneration. The mind has been slowly coming to this point all through that series of states and experiences which were described, in symbolic forms of expression, by the various things brought into being during the six days of creation. Each new thing created was, in this higher meaning, descriptive of some added principle, newer thought, freshly developed capacity, holier affection, diviner love, brought forth on the field of the mind.

And on the seventh day God ended his work which he had made. As all allusions here are spiritual, the work of God is his work of recreating or regenerating the human mind. When that is complete his work is ended. But we must here avoid the idea of work which pertains to the labors of man. It is not a wrestling with a perverse human understanding and heart. It is not toil and strife and strained exertion. The Lord's energies proceed in quietness. They go forth after the gentle manner of sunbeams, and they develop minds with the noiseless methods by which plants grow and buds expand and fruits ripen. Whatever of unrest there is, whatever of wrestle and toil and strife, is on the man's part.

While regeneration is progressing there is more or less inward opposition to the hoped-for change. The earthly nature rebels against spiritual views of things, spiritual methods of action, the government of the nature by the spiritual law of right and wrong. The regenerative influences of the Lord are often, as it were, swept back. The good and the bad enter into a struggle for the mastery. Or, it would be better to say, the bad struggles to prevent the good from assuming the control. All who have ever sought to do the right in the face of a temptation to do the wrong, know the nature of those contests which occur on the arena of the mind. All who have held mistaken views of things, and have afterwards come into the light of truth, know of the mental combats by which they are released from the one and gain conviction of the other.

Suppose a new truth is presented which conflicts with long cherished opinions. The earthly nature opposes it; the higher urges its acceptance. The natural mind bristles with opposition; the spiritual seeks to show its rationality. It is almost like a debate between different persons. The *pros* and *cons* are urged with force and effect on either side. Any one will observe this who will but take the trouble to think. Doing so, he cannot but conclude that the mind has two lines of thought—one spiritual, the other natural; one false, the other true; two impulses—one for the good, the other for the bad; one toward heaven, the other toward the world; two minds, as it were—the one for the contemplation of spiritual themes, for the understanding of spiritual truths, for the love and practice of a spiritual life, the other for the pursuit of worldly affairs, for the acquirement of worldly knowledge and for the delights which inhere in a worldly life. When one begins to strive for the higher way, these two elements come into conflict. On the mind's plane of thought and reason, they argue and debate. On the plane of affection, they enter into combat. On the plane of outward action, they come into mutual disagreement. In the conflict thus induced, at times the one prevails, at times the other; now it is the spiritual mind which gains the ascendency, and again it is the natural which wins the day.

The combat goes on between these two elements of the nature, all along the path of the regeneration. Indeed, without it regeneration were impossible. When we gain some light concerning the higher life, the very opposition to it of the lower nature shows us what we are. When we learn the true character of unselfishness, the opposition of the natural mind to its high behests reveals the selfishness to which we cling. Until we know ourselves we cannot rise. Until we know wherein we are wrong we cannot go right. Now all the decisions of the natural man—his ends, thoughts and acts, come from the lower mind. But all that is spiritual, in will, thought or deed, is the influence of the Lord flowing into the spiritual mind, and moving it to assert its supremacy. So while this struggle goes on, God's work goes on. But when, at last, the natural mind yields, and is brought into obedience to, and harmony with, the higher nature, then there is no more opposition, no more debate, no more combat; the Lord's influences press unresisted in with the happy consent of the entire mind. While the former state is called the work of God, this is termed the rest of God. Therefore it is said, "On the seventh day God ended his work which he had made; and he rested on the seventh day from all his work which he had made."

So God's rest is also man's rest. When man attains this state, he doubts no more concerning spiritual truth; he hesitates no more as to the path of good. His rationality concerning spiritual things becomes so quickened and so strengthened, that they act as intuitions on the mind. His sensitiveness to evil, or to the very shadow or breath of wrong, becomes so exquisite and delicate, that it is shrunk from with the spontaneous energy with which one would snatch his hand from contact with a scorpion. Indeed, he comes into a condition wherein he loves truth and good, and that of a spiritual kind, for their own sakes, so well, that they come to him with all the force of things that cannot be questioned. He would as soon question the sun in the radiance of his shining, the light as it lit before his very eyes the path of his going, the warmth whose genial glow filled every pleasurable sense with joy, as to question God, truth or goodness as they become realized things to the love of the soul, the light of the understanding, and the experience of his life.

Do you know that there is such a thing as certainty in respect to things your bodily eyes have never seen? If you do not, you have missed the enjoyment of the most exquisite sense with which the Creator has endowed the soul. But you do, if you will only step down from, and out of, your sense of self-sufficiency, and consent to believe what you know. Can the poet's sensibility detect a flaw in the rhythmic measure of a line, the artist's eye descry the untrue in the drawing of a picture, the musician's ear discover the slightest deviation from exact harmony in a band of a hundred pieces, and this by the intuition of a moment, and the spiritual nature have no instant intuitions of its own—no ear for the true, no sense for the good, that is as undeviating as the lines of light? But, you say, the intuition of the poet, the artist, or the musician comes by cultivation. And is it true that God has made our natural faculties so wondrously sensitive to cultivation, and left our spiritual faculties, do what we may, dulled and blunted, and inoblivious to the very things for the cultivation of which they were designed? Believe it not. When you do not detect by instantaneous intuition the false sound of error if it strikes upon the ear, nor grasp in its very utterance the truth of God, it is because your spiritual ear is unattuned to the harmonies of heaven; when you do not sense the instant presence of evil in its lightest breath across the heart, and know the voice of good by its very sound of rhythmic harmony, by its very sphere of sweetness to the soul, it is because your sensibility to the influences of the one eternal loving One are dull and apathetic. There is a state of mind where error is as easily recognized as the baleful shadow of the night, and truth as easily seen as the light in its summer shining; where evil is as sensitively recognized as the cold of the polar zone, and good as exquisitely perceived as the sweet, soft airs of a perfect spring. To cultivate this is the object of regeneration. No excellence in the whole realm of existence is obtained without cultivation. Full regeneration, the seventh day of the new creation, is the perfection of the spiritual nature. Truth is then a perception, good an intuition. We work no more to find them; we labor no more to obtain them; they are ours by right of the manhood established within; they are ours as heirs of God.

Here, and in this state, there is perfect rest of mind. This is not rest in the sense of no more learning, or aspiring, or doing. It is rest from inward opposition or doubt. Indeed, the field of truth, especially on spiritual lines, is so broad and deep, and high, that the mind can never cease to earn. Rest, in this spiritual sense, is absence of worry. Rest in the sense of inertness is utterly abhorrent to the true manhood of man. And there is peace for the heart. There is no more enticement to sin. No doubts of right or wrong arise at any given point. The perfect way is as patent as the broad avenues, which none may mistake, to the natural feet of man. We have learned to know the Lord and to love Him, and the breath of his celestial presence permeates with the sphere of love all things of life. Nothing can disturb us; nothing molest. The magic wand of perfect trust in his overshadowing love in all life's comings and goings, brushes away the annoyances of life at every step and state.

This is the rest of God. Not only is it so in the sense of his resting from the work of overcoming opposition to his entrances in the spirit, but in that of his absolute repose on mind and heart, as gently as the sunbeams rest on the summer earth. This state is described by our Lord himself in his words to his disciples, "Abide in me and I in you; as the branch cannot bear fruit of itself except it abide in the vine, no more can ye except ye abide in me."

Swedenborg has called this state the celestial state as distinguished from the spiritual. We may be spiritual men, but we have always then a higher life to labor for. Indeed from the very day that the firmament is created within, that is, from the time when the firmament of spiritual thought and purpose is formed above the earthly mind, be it in ever so small a degree, we begin to be spiritual. But in the celestial state there is no more regenerative work to labor over, because the work of regeneration is already accomplished. We are not, however, inactive. Rest does not mean idleness. Peace does not require us to sit with folded hands. We will not retire to caves, away from the companionship of man, to contemplate the glory of God. Indeed, the celestial man is the most enquiring, the most active, the most zealous, the most persevering of all. But he labors for good. He loves his neighbor as himself; but in the other world where he need not labor for his own food and raiment, he loves his neighbor better than himself. True, work he does. But that which he once called work is pleasure now. This is because his delight is in being useful; and all labor which has its end in use is no longer labor in the sense of toil, but is rest. So, with the celestial man, his rest is activity, his peace is energy, his work is pleasure, his love of use the very happiness of life, and his love of God the ceaseless affection of his heart for all that light of truth and impulse of good, which flows from the Divine Being into his receptive nature.

Thus it is that *God blessed the seventh day and sanctified it, because that in it he had rested from all his work which God created and made.* As the seventh day represents the celestial state—the state of rest and peace, when evil no longer tempts and the spirits of sin seduce no more, unquestionably it is blessed. Certainly it is sanctified or made holy. We must understand that no natural thing is holy in itself. It is sanctified by reason of the spiritual principle within. No one day, in itself considered, is more holy than another. It becomes so only by virtue of what it represents. It remains so only in consideration of the holy use to which, by virtue of that representation, it is put. There are six successive states or stages during which the work or struggle or combat of regeneration is performed. The seventh state is holy because combat has ceased and the man has surrendered himself to the Lord.

It was not, therefore, because the earth was literally created in six days, which it was not, and God rested on the seventh, that the Sabbath was instituted. The spiritual meaning of the seventh day of creation is carried over consistently into the Sabbath commandment. It is because the seventh day is the type and representation of a finished regenerate nature that the Sabbath was proclaimed. All memorial days are sacred because of that which they commemorate. As mere arbitrary holidays they would be valueless. But put a meaning into them and they become something. They are then ever recurring lessons. They are memorials of something worth remembering. The fourth of July commemorates the birth of liberty. Its observance keeps alive the virtue of patriotism on the altar of the national soul. Christmas recalls the birth of Christ. It directs vivid attention to the grandest event in the cycles of sacred history. The Sabbath, in its real and primal meaning, commemorates the doctrine of the rebirth of the soul—its completed regeneration. But while the first mentioned were human institutions, the Sabbath was ordained by the Lord. It is, therefore, sacred, and calls for a proper observance in a sense far higher than the others.

Men dispute over the natural day, as to which one should be recognized as the true Sabbath. It is a matter of little or no consequence. Whether it is the first day of the week, or the last or the middle one is of no moment, if for no other reason, because the week as a division of time is a human and not a divine institution. I mean by this, that the Lord, although He commanded us to keep each recurring seventh day, issued no ordinance setting forth the division of days into weeks, and instituting this day as the first and that as the last. There is no commandment which reads, "Remember the last day of the week to keep it holy," nor is there any precept which says, "Remember Saturday,

Sunday or Friday, to keep it holy." There is no allusion, indeed, to the week in any way. It is simply said, "Six day shalt thou labor and do all thy work, but the seventh day is the Sabbath— that is the rest—of the Lord thy God." We are to keep one day in seven in commemoration of the grand celestial institution of a perfect regeneration for man. Any natural day will do so long as a seventh day is kept. But as its uses would be immeasurably decreased by every individual setting for himself a different day, it is palpably right for the common consent of the church to decide the question.

Sabbath means rest. Sabbath day is rest day. It means that as the seventh state of regeneration is complete rest from selfishness and worldliness, and a perfect surrender to the Lord, a regular recurring seventh day must be kept in memory of that fact. At that time we must rest, as much as possible, from worldly business, from worldly thoughts, from worldly schemes, in order that we may worship the Lord, reflect upon spiritual things, learn spiritual truths, and form resolutions of spiritual life. This is a rest from the world and self that helps us on toward heaven. The Sabbath was given for the spiritual benefit of man. Is it wicked then to break the Sabbath? It is not a question of sin. It is simply this: that they who do not keep the

Sabbath for the purposes for which it was given will lose the spiritual benefits for which it was designed. Immersed, day in and day out, with no spiritual rest of mind, in business, in pleasure, in dissipation, in the thousand worldly things which draw our thoughts away from heaven, they will lose their way in the path of regeneration, and thus fail to reach the goal for which each and all were born.

But we approach the end of our task. That task has been to unfold the true meaning of this first chapter of Genesis. What have we found to be its value? Was it especially given to teach that God made the earth and the starry heavens? That is written all over the face of the holy Scriptures. It is inscribed in living light every where upon the face of the universe. Nay, its specific use is to teach us a lesson of lessons. It is one which the world heeds not, but from which he who *will* heed shall obtain blessings beyond the power of language to express.

The lesson is this: that man, in the order of his creation, is ushered upon the plane of earth in mental darkness and great voidness of soul. It is the design of the Lord that he shall be elevated from this condition, and that he shall be recreated into the Divine image and likeness. He has a part in this himself. The Lord gives the truth, but he must rationally receive it. The Lord presents the good, but he must voluntarily do it. The Lord sends love to his heart, but he must love it out to his fellow man. The Lord clothes his understanding with wisdom, but he must do his deeds of love with the wise insight that wisdom gives. The Lord operates for man's regeneration, but he must cooperate. If the Lord sends light to the chambers of his mind, he must throw open the windows of the soul that the light may flow in. If the Lord sends spiritual warmth, he must stand in the presence of his shining, and not lose its benefits by plunging into the fogs and shadows of self, where the benignant sun cannot reach.

So as man begins his career in darkness the Lord sends light. "Let there be light!" is the Divine fiat, and childhood is filled with schools and books and parental teachings to the dispersion of the shadows of life's beginnings. "Let there be a firmament in heaven!" and slowly the mind, prepared by the light of God, opens in its higher firmaments of heavenly thought, so that it may be capable of being filled with comprehensions of spiritual things. "Let there be first tender growths of herb and fruit!" and the spirit is clothed with the verdant germs of a better life, and the fruits of truer action are pendant on the bending boughs of its tree of life. "Let sun, moon and stars appear upon the firmament!" and love, faith and knowledge, spiritually realized, and rationally seen—the great lights of the heavenly mind, illumine its higher regions with thoughts, hopes and aspirations, and glorious glimpses of the higher life, which bathe the brightening world of the soul with joy. "Let the waters bring forth the living soul!" and from the great reservoirs of the mind, its waters of spiritual truth, start forth conceptions of God, heaven and eternal life, which make the soul a living, sentient thing, in a sense of which hitherto it has not dreamed. "Let the earth bring forth the living creature—cattle, beast and creeping thing!" and lo, the affections of the higher nature, of which these forms of living life are the symbols, become grandly alive toward God and man. "Let us make man in our image!" and the soul, now thoroughly transformed, becomes, in all its forms and full activities, in its very organism, in its every impulse, thought and act, an image of its Maker, the very and the only Man. "Let there be rest from creation's work, and the seventh day remain forever sanctified!" and the once weary soul is blessed, in this its high estate, with rest from evil, and peace in its completed state of love, while the holiness of God broods over all its walks and ways. Then supernal wisdom lights the human path of life, love in its manifestations of never ending beauty is the very life of its throbbing energies, truth lights the mind with never dying fires, and goodness crowns its little universe of action with joy and gladness.

Thus does regeneration become a work of orderly progress and successive growth. Guided by the Lord, it is brought forward under his never ceasing energies. It is begun in chaos and ends in the glorious likeness of Divinity. This, and manifold more, the parable of the Creation sets forth, in its beautiful symbols, concerning the beginnings of the soul, its progress through the stages of its advancing career, the nature of each successive state, and the quality of its celestial outcomes. It is a lovely picture of the elevations of life to which we may dare aspire, a perfect delineation of the path we are divinely called to tread, a chart of life by which we may safely work our way, a glorious promise of our heavenly future if we are but true.

We may learn concerning science in the rock-ribbed earth, and trace the courses of the stars by the mathematics learned of man. But the Word of God is given that He may reveal Himself amid the weary ways of earth, build eternal hopes in the heart of fallen man, point the path to the higher life which reigns in heaven, and bathe the soul with the love and truth Divine. So only is the holy Scripture justified; so only our hearts made happy in its study; so only eternal life made sure through its leaves of wonderful light.

www.ingramcontent.com/pod-product-compliance
Lightning Source LLC
Chambersburg PA
CBHW030248170426
43202CB00009B/667